2015

100
BEST QUICK
GLUTEN-FREE
RECIPES

CAROL FENSTER

PHOTOGRAPHS BY
JASON WYCHE

HOUGHTON MIFFLIN HARCOURT
BOSTON • NEW YORK • 2014

Copyright © 2014 by Carol Fenster

Interior photography © 2014 by Jason Wyche

www.hmhco.com

Library of Congress Cataloging-in-Publication Data

Fenster, Carol Lee.
100 best quick gluten-free recipes / Carol Fenster.
pages cm
Includes index.
ISBN 978-0-544-26371-0 (hardcover); 978-0-544-26379-6 (ebk)

1. Gluten-free diet—Recipes. 2. Quick and easy cooking. I. Title. II. Title: One hundred
best quick gluten-free recipes.
RM237.86.F4523 2014
641.5'12—dc23
2013044982

Printed in China

C&C 10 9 8 7 6 5 4 3 2 1

Publisher: Natalie Chapman
Executive Editor: Linda Ingroia
Assistant Editor: Molly Aronica
Production Editors: Jacqueline Beach and Helen Seachrist
Cover Design: Chrissy Kurpeski
Interior Design and Layout: Waterbury Publications, Inc., Des Moines, IA
Manufacturing Manager: Kevin Watt

Acknowledgments

I want to thank the staff at Houghton Mifflin Harcourt, especially my fabulous editor, Linda Ingroia—who suggested and worked with me on this book and its predecessor, 1,000 Gluten-Free Recipes. Her assistant, Molly Aronica, was very helpful, and I appreciate the great work of the production editor, Jacqueline Beach, and designer Ken Carlson of Waterbury. My photo "dream team"—photographer Jason Wyche, food stylist Chelsea Zimmer, and prop stylist Kira Corbin— did a beautiful job of making my food look real and delicious.

I am also grateful for the ongoing support of my fantastic agent, Lisa Ekus, and her staff. I am fortunate to work with many outstanding professional colleagues in the gluten-free community, and my readers are the absolute best. I extend my love to my family—Larry, Brett, Helke, Keene, Romi, and Cole—and my gratitude for their support.

Author's Note

The 100 recipes in this book are largely from the award-winning 1,000 Gluten-Free Recipes—a colossal, 3½-pound tome that is the largest gluten-free cookbook in the world—although I enhanced and updated many of those recipes and added new recipes. Plus, the recipes here are in a beautiful, handy package and feature gorgeous photos! My goal for this much smaller—but incredibly useful—book is to help you get a meal on the table in less than 30 minutes. You'll find easy, streamlined dinner recipes, plus breakfasts, lunches, snacks, sides, and desserts—each designed to reduce the stress of making a gluten-free meal for yourself, your family, or guests that will satisfy everyone. I love writing gluten-free cookbooks because they make it possible for gluten-free people to enjoy delicious food, just like everyone else. This lovely little book is the perfect gift for your gluten-free friends, family, and of course, for yourself. Bon appétit—without wheat!

Contents

Introduction

It's a common late-afternoon or evening refrain: "What's for dinner?" Consumer research says that it's the most stressful time of the day for families who want healthy meals but have little time. Gluten-free? That just makes it more complicated, because gluten-free families often prepare most of their meals rather than dining out to avoid inadvertently eating gluten.

However, having followed the gluten-free lifestyle for more than 25 years now, I feel well qualified to say that if there ever was a time to be gluten-free—and not have the quest for safe food dominate our lives—it is now. The Food and Drug Administration (FDA) in 2013 identified the guidelines for gluten-free food labeling. And there is rapidly expanding acknowledgment by food manufacturers and food market owners of the growing need for gluten-free foods. In fact, the market for gluten-free foods is expected to reach $6.6 billion by 2017. Gluten-free is big business! This book will help you take advantage of this progress to quickly get meals on the table.

What Is Gluten?

From a baker's perspective, gluten is a component of wheat flour that provides wonderful elasticity in bread dough but can toughen piecrusts and biscuits if the dough is handled too much.

Scientifically, gluten is a naturally occurring protein in wheat and related grains such as barley, rye, kamut, spelt, and triticale. It wasn't long ago that oats were also on this list. Oats do not inherently contain gluten, but they were previously banished from the gluten-free diet because of possible contamination with wheat in the field or during processing. Today, several companies offer pure, uncontaminated gluten-free oats, but check with your physician first to make sure they're right for you.

Why Can't Some People Eat Gluten?

CELIAC DISEASE

Celiac disease is an inherited autoimmune disorder that affects the digestive process of the small intestine. When gluten is eaten, the hair-like cilia that line the small intestine and absorb nutrients from food become inflamed and eventually flatten, thus inhibiting the absorption of important nutrients into the body.

Dr. Alessio Fasano, medical director of the Center for Celiac Research, says that approximately 1 in 133 Americans—ten times more than originally thought—has celiac disease, and he calls it the "most prevalent genetically transmitted condition in the world." This means that nearly three million Americans are living with this condition.

Unlike many other diseases, there is no pill, no vaccine, and no surgical procedure to cure celiac disease. The only treatment is a lifelong gluten-free diet. If gluten is ingested, the intestines are damaged even if one doesn't exhibit the typical symptoms of diarrhea, bloating, gas, or fatigue. In fact, experts say that roughly one-third to one-half of celiac patients do not exhibit these typical symptoms.

Celiac disease must be managed with the help of a gastroenterologist, who performs a series of tests—possibly including a small-bowel endoscopy while the patient is sedated—before a final diagnosis is made. For more information on celiac disease, see Sources (page 187).

NON-CELIAC GLUTEN SENSITIVITY

Dr. Fasano coined the term non-celiac gluten-sensitivity as a label for those of us (6 to 7 percent, or between 18 and 21 million Americans) who don't have celiac disease but are still sickened by gluten. I am in this category. My response to gluten was brain fog, fatigue, and nasal congestion and stuffiness—often resulting in sinus infections that lasted for up to a year at a time. Then the antibiotics required to treat them were another blow to my system, and sinus surgery to correct all the damage from the infections was yet another setback. Other people have stomachaches, headaches, rashes, joint aches—to name just a few symptoms. Consuming gluten may not kill those of us with gluten sensitivity (or gluten intolerance, as it's also called), but it certainly compromises the quality of our lives.

ALLERGIES

According to Food Allergy and Research Education (formerly Food Allergy & Anaphylaxis Network, at www.foodallergy.org), about 15 million Americans suffer from true food allergies, and wheat is one of the top eight food allergens. True food allergies involve the immune system's IgE antibodies, and reactions are usually sudden and more pronounced. Few people have true allergies to wheat, but for those who do, it's very, very serious. Diagnosis of a food allergy should be made by a board-certified allergist or a health professional.

AUTISM AND OTHER CONDITIONS

According to www.autismspeaks.org, approximately 1 in 88 children (1 in 54 boys) are estimated to have autism, a neurobiological disorder that seems to be rising and perplexes families and the medical community alike. As part of the overall treatment (but not as a substitute for other treatment or as a cure), several experts advocate a gluten-free, casein-free diet (casein is a milk protein), because some autistic children do not process these proteins properly and removing them from the diet helps their behavior. While many families use my gluten-free/casein-free recipes for their autistic children, you and your physician should decide whether this diet is right for your child. For more information on autism and the gluten-free/casein-free diet, consult go to www.gfcfdiet.com or www.autismspeaks.org.

Other medical conditions, such as food-triggered asthma, may warrant a gluten-free diet. Sometimes a gluten-free diet is part of the treatment (but not a cure) for certain autoimmune conditions. Ask your physician about whether a gluten-free diet is appropriate for you. Remember, it is not a weight-loss diet; neither is it a good idea to try it without an official diagnosis, because you might omit important nutrients when fortified foods such as bread, pasta, and wheat cereal are avoided. That's why it is so important to get the advice of a dietitian or nutritionist. And it is always important to monitor calories, fat, and portion sizes, so I provide nutrient analysis for each recipe.

Notes: These recipes were not developed to fit within any official dietary guidelines but rather to provide a variety of options for foods you love or will enjoy trying, and they incorporate a range of ingredients for a varied, balanced diet. You should keep track of your own dietary needs and use or adapt the recipes as you like. Also, note that the nutrition information includes only the required ingredients in the recipes, not the optional ingredients. I use 1% milk.

TIME IN THE KITCHEN

We all get 24 hours in a day, but gluten-free families spend a proportionately larger share of that day devoted to food preparation. Between busy work and school schedules, family commitments, and extracurricular activities, it's hard to carve out time in the kitchen and avoid that late-afternoon "refrigerator stare-down." This book will help you by offering safe, delicious, healthy recipes with ingredients and techniques that use your kitchen time efficiently to quickly prepare a safe, tasty meal.

The recipes in this book demonstrate several ways to save time in the kitchen. Almost all of these recipes can be made in less than 30 minutes. Of course, the first time you make a dish, it may take extra time to get used to certain techniques or to get comfortable cooking with certain ingredients. How your stove and oven function may also influence cooking time. And some recipes may take a little longer than 30 minutes, such as the French baguettes, but overall they are quite quick compared to the traditional recipes. You will save enough time that you'll want to keep these recipes in your go-to repertoire for simple, efficient, satisfying dishes.

The recipes in this book demonstrate several ways to save time in the kitchen, such as using:

- A plan-ahead approach. Make sure your pantry is stocked with versatile, flavorful gluten-free ingredients that are ready when you need them. Cook extra food ahead of time (for example, make two casseroles: one for tonight and another for the freezer). Prepare more than you need for tonight's meal, such as extra diced onions, green peppers, or celery, and freeze the surplus for a future meal. Or, cook extra whole grains or brown rice and refrigerate or freeze for later. Prepare a larger cut of meat or poultry than you need for one meal—such as pork shoulder or roast chicken. Serve some tonight and freeze the rest for use in future dishes such as casseroles, stews, tacos, or wraps.

- One bold-flavored ingredient instead of several ingredients to save precious measuring time, such as store-bought seasoning blends that replace several individual flavoring agents. Or, store-bought Mexican salsa instead of homemade versions for Southwestern dishes or store-bought teriyaki sauce for Asian dishes.

- Cooking techniques that free you to work on one part of the meal while other parts cook, such as pan roasting (where meat is browned in a skillet and then placed in the oven to finish roasting untended).

- Smaller containers to shorten cooking time, such as cooking meat loaf in cupcake pans rather than 5x9-inch loaf pans or baking quick breads in 4x6-inch mini pans rather than 4x8-inch loaf pans.

- Appliances that cook untended, such as slow cookers for soups or rice cookers for rice.

- Appliances that reduce overall cooking time, such as the microwave for making polenta, rather than stirring it on the stovetop. Or, microwave a single breakfast muffin in a minute rather than baking several in the oven for 25 minutes.

How to Use This Book

This book is divided into five chapters:
Breakfast and Breads
Soups, Salads, Sandwiches, and Snacks
Grains, Beans, and Pasta
Main Dishes
Desserts

Within each chapter, you will find a wide selection of quick recipes, with an icon ● to indicate vegetarian recipes.

Read this Introduction thoroughly before you start cooking. It explains which basic ingredients to stock in a gluten-free pantry, background information on flours and grains used in these recipes, and which gluten-free brands of ingredients were used in developing the recipes. It also explains how to measure ingredients accurately, a step that is critical to success in gluten-free baking.

The recipe chapters also include helpful sidebars that further detail certain ingredients or offer tips for saving time. As a bonus, gluten-free menus for a variety of occasions, ranging from everyday to special, are provided. A list of Sources on page 187 includes helpful Web sites for more information on diet, medical conditions, labeling, foods, dining out, travel, research, testing, and many other things you might want to know about the gluten-free diet.

SAFETY IN THE GLUTEN-FREE KITCHEN

You spend lots of time carefully choosing safe ingredients in the grocery store. But your responsibility doesn't stop there. It's just as important to handle those ingredients safely at home to ensure that they remain gluten-free. Here are just a few of the precautions that will increase the safety of your food.

- Use separate knives, cutting boards, and serving utensils for gluten-free foods. A knife used to spread butter on wheat bread can transfer wheat particles back to the butter. Wheat bread can leave crumbs on a cutting board, and that can contaminate gluten-free bread if it's cut right afterward on the same board. A spoon used to serve both couscous and then plain white rice will contaminate the rice. A knife used to cut a wheat-bread sandwich should not be used to cut a gluten-free sandwich, unless it's carefully washed and dried first.

- Use separate appliances when there is the possibility of cross-contamination. For example, wheat-bread crumbs in a toaster may touch gluten-free bread during toasting. Food residue can collect in appliance crevices, such as in bread machines (where the kneading blade inserts), and these crevices may harbor wheat particles. The same is true for blenders (the area where the blade attaches) and electric mixers (the area where the beaters insert into the mixer). If you must use the same appliance, carefully clean it between uses.
- Minimize particles of wheat flour in the air when sifting or measuring if your kitchen is not dedicated to gluten-free baking. Carefully wipe down all kitchen surfaces after baking with wheat flour (or regular oats, barley, spelt, or rye) to remove any particles that settle there after baking. Better yet, follow these measures and then wait 24 hours so the airborne particles have settled, and then wipe down again.
- Store gluten-free food in clearly marked, tightly sealed containers on shelves or in areas designated as gluten-free to avoid accidental ingestion.

THE GLUTEN-FREE PANTRY

When you're new to the gluten-free diet, deciding what to stock in your pantry can seem perplexing. First, check out the recipes in this book and decide which ones you want to make, and note the ingredients they require. Then, look over the lists in Brands Used in Testing These Recipes (page 17) and also the lists in Flours and Grains Used in This Book (page 13). If you keep those items on hand, you'll always be ready to cook. In addition, here are some basics that you will always need to keep on hand:

- xanthan gum and guar gum for baking
- active dry yeast for baking
- baking soda and baking powder for baking
- salt, pepper, and pure spices for seasoning
- pickles, ketchup, mayonnaise, mustard, and relish
- canned or frozen fruits and vegetables
- canned or dried beans and legumes
- perishables such as eggs, milk, juices, fruits, and vegetables

FLOURS AND GRAINS USED IN THIS BOOK

All of the recipes in this book are made with gluten-free ingredients. If you are new to the gluten-free lifestyle, you might be unfamiliar with some of the gluten-free flours and grains we use in preparing food. Many "grains" are actually seeds of plants, but we call them grains for simplicity. Some flours are ground from vegetables, beans, or nuts instead of grains. In several cases, such as oats or brown rice, we use both the flour and the grain. Here is a quick overview.

	Description	Available as
Almond meal/flour	Ground from whole almonds (for meal) or slivered almonds (for flour).	Whole (nut) or flour/meal
Amaranth	Ancient grain once grown by the Aztecs for its superior nutrients. Related to pigweed.	Whole grain or flour
Brown rice	Unpolished whole rice kernel, including bran, germ, and endosperm. When polished, becomes white rice.	Whole grain or flour
Buckwheat	Not wheat, but the seed of a plant related to rhubarb. Toasted groats are called kasha.	Whole grain or flour
Cornmeal (yellow)	Meal ground from whole corn kernels. Corn flour can also be ground from whole corn kernels.	Flour or meal
Cornstarch	Ground from corn and used as flour to lighten baked goods or as thickener for sauces, gravies, and soups.	Flour
Hemp seed	Easily digested, high-protein hulled seeds; added to baked goods like nuts or ground into protein powder for smoothies.	Whole (nut) or powder. Powder can also be used as flour in baking.
Millet	Seed of a grass related to sorghum. Prized for its easily digested (alkaline) protein.	Whole grain or flour
Oats* + (groats)	Whole oat kernels; no bran removed. (If bran is removed, the bran is sold separately as oat bran. If whole oat groats are chopped, the chopped groats are sold as steel-cut oats.)	Whole grain or flour
Oats* + (rolled)	Whole oat kernels steamed and flattened (rolled) and commonly used to make breakfast oatmeal.	Whole grain
Potato starch	Ground from peeled dried potatoes. Used to lighten baked goods and thicken sauces and soups.	Flour

continued on page 14

continued from page 13

	Description	Available as
Quinoa	Known as mother grain due to its superior nutrients; ancient seed once cultivated by Incas in Peru. Related to spinach.	Whole grain or flour
Rice bran	Outer hull from brown rice kernel; used in foods for its high fiber and protein.	Rice bran particles or flour
Sorghum	World's fifth largest cereal crop; seed of a grass from Asia and Africa but also grown in central United States. Distantly related to maize.	Whole grain or flour
Sweet rice flour	Ground from white sticky rice (sometimes called glutinous rice) but contains no wheat gluten. Often used in sushi. Flour adds pliability to baked goods; excellent thickener for soups and gravies.	Whole grain or flour
Tapioca	Ground from manioc or cassava root; adds "chew" and crustiness in baked goods.	Whole grain (tapioca granules for pudding) or flour
Teff	Teff, a cereal grass, means "tiny" and comes from Ethiopia, where it is a staple and often used in injera bread.	Whole grain or flour
Wild rice	Not rice, but the seed of an aquatic grass commonly grown in the northern United States.	Whole grain or flour

*Available from www.bobsredmill.com, www.creamhillestates.com, www.giftsofnature.net, www.glutenfreeoats.com, or www.onlyoats.com.

+Check with your physician before using gluten-free oats.

The recipes in this book rely on Carol's Sorghum Blend, an extremely versatile blend of flours that can be used as the basis for many dishes. If you keep the following blend in your pantry, you'll always be prepared to bake.

Carol's Sorghum Blend

MAKES: 4 CUPS

1½ **cups sorghum flour (or brown rice flour)**
1½ **cups potato starch or cornstarch**
 1 **cup tapioca flour**

Whisk the ingredients together until well blended. Store, tightly covered, in a dark, dry place. You may refrigerate or freeze the blend, but bring to room temperature before using. You may double or triple the recipe. Using brown rice flour instead of sorghum flour produces baked goods that are somewhat lighter in texture and color.

MEASURING FOR SUCCESS

It is very important to measure flour carefully. All of the recipes in my books measure flour this way: Whisk the flour a few times to aerate or fluff it up and then lightly spoon it into a measuring cup before leveling it off with a knife. Don't use the measuring cup as a scoop and don't pack the flour down; you'll get up to 20 percent more flour that way, and that can cause a failure. Use spouted measuring cups only for liquids because it's hard to determine an accurate amount of flour in them. To see flour measured, see Videos at www.carolfenster.com.

I use standard brands of flours purchased in natural food stores or supermarkets. I don't use superfine flours, such as those from Asian markets, since they absorb liquids differently than the standard brands. I don't grind my own flours because I need the consistency of store-bought flours to make sure the recipe works the same way each and every time.

SAVVY LABEL READING

It is very important to choose gluten-free ingredients carefully. The Food Allergen Labeling and Consumer Protection Act of 2004 (FALCPA) makes shopping easier because the phrase

"Contains: Wheat" must appear on any food that contains wheat. But it is extremely important to read the labels each time you buy because manufacturers can change procedures or ingredients at any time. Also, the law only requires the warning about wheat, not the other gluten-containing grains such as barley, rye, spelt, kamut, triticale, and non-gluten-free oats—but they will be in the ingredient list, so you will know whether that food is safe or not. If the ingredient list contains oats but does not specify gluten-free oats, don't eat it.

In 2013, the FDA defined *gluten-free* as a product with "less than 20 parts per million (ppm) of gluten." There is no requirement that gluten-free foods be labeled as gluten-free, but when a manufacturer chooses to put *gluten-free* on food packaging, the item must comply with the FDA definition.

To further help you identify safe foods, the Gluten-Free Certification Organization (a branch of the Gluten Intolerance Group) certifies companies as gluten-free and authorizes them to display a certification logo on the food item. The Celiac Support Association and the National Foundation for Celiac Awareness also offer certification programs. Companies that don't use these logos don't necessarily manufacture unsafe foods, but these logos are yet another tool for you to use when you shop.

GLUTEN-FREE, DAIRY-FREE INGREDIENTS

All of the recipes in this book are gluten-free, but they can be made dairy-free as well. To help you locate gluten-free, dairy-free versions of certain ingredients, here is a list of the brands I used in testing these recipes. Whenever I use an ingredient that is available in both gluten-containing and gluten-free brands (such as soy sauce), I specify *gluten-free,* as in *gluten-free soy sauce,* in the ingredient list. If a recipe calls for a gluten-free ingredient, you should look at the chart below to find the gluten-free brand I used; however, you may find other gluten-free brands in your store.

All of these recipes can be made with dairy substitutes, so the chart also lists dairy-free brands. But, as noted, you must continue to read labels, since manufacturers may change ingredients or manufacturing practices, which could change the gluten-free status of a food or ingredient. I use 1% milk.

BRANDS USED IN TESTING THESE RECIPES

This list of ingredients is not an endorsement of these companies; they are the brands used when I developed the recipes in this book. They were gluten-free at the time, but always read labels before buying any food or ingredient to make sure it is gluten-free. Manufacturers can change ingredients or manufacturing practices, making a gluten-free product no longer safe. Also, some manufacturers use similar packages for their gluten-containing and gluten-free products, so reading the labels is necessary to distinguish between the two.

Food or Ingredient	Gluten-Free Brand(s)
Baking and Cooking Aids	
Butterscotch morsels	HyVee, Safeway, Shurfine
Chocolate chips	Tropical Source/SunSpire, Enjoy Life Foods, Ghirardelli
Chocolate cookies	Pamela's Double Chocolate Chocolate Chip
Cookie crumbs	Pamela's cookies
Dry milk powder	Organic Valley
Dry milk powder substitute	Better Than Milk
Espresso powder	Medaglia D'oro
Guar gum	Bob's Red Mill
Shortening (non-hydrogenated)	Spectrum, Earth Balance, Crisco
Unflavored gelatin powder	Knox, Grayslake
White chocolate chips	Tropical Source/SunSpire
Xanthan gum	Bob's Red Mill
Beverages and Drinks	
Beer	Bard's Tale, Green's, New Grist, New Planet, Redbridge, Ramapo Valley
Almond Milk	Silk
Coconut Milk	So Delicious
Flaxseed Milk	Flaxmilk
Hazelnut Milk	Pacific Natural Foods
Hemp Milk	Living Harvest
Rice Milk	Rice Dream
Soy Milk	Silk
Sunflower Milk	SoL or Sunsational

Bread, Tortillas, Pizza, Crackers

Corn tortillas	Mission
Crackers (savory)	Edward & Sons, Mary's Gone Crackers, Flackers, Crunchmaster
Flour tortillas	Rudi's is preferred, but also Food for Life, La Tortilla Factory
English muffins	Food for Life
Graham crackers	Kinnikinnick
Hamburger buns	Canyon Bakehouse, Udi's, Rudi's
Italian breadsticks (grissini)	Dr. Schär
Pizza crust	Against the Grain, Whole Foods
Polenta tube	Food Merchant
Rice bran crackers	Health Valley
Sandwich bread	Rudi's, Udi's, Whole Foods, Canyon Bakehouse
Tostada shells	Mission

Candy, Desserts, Toppings, Sauces

Chocolate syrup	Hershey's
Vanilla pudding	Kozy Shack
Whipped topping	Lucerne, Soyatoo
White chocolate chips	Hershey's, Tropical Source/SunSpire

Cereal, Crackers, Pizza

Brown rice crisps	Erewhon, Barbara's
Cornflakes	Nature's Path, Erewhon
Puffed rice cereal	Erewhon, Kellogg's, Kinnikinnick
Pizza crust	Against the Grain, Udi's

Condiments, Savory Sauces, Dips

Asian seasoning	Spice Islands garam masala, McCormick Perfect Pinch Asian
Asian fish sauce	A Taste of Thai, Thai Kitchen
Asian spice blend	McCormick Perfect Pinch
Barbecue sauce	Cattlemen's, Heinz Regular
Basil pesto	Shaw's, Safeway Select
Bean dip	Fritos
Beau monde seasoning	Spice Islands
Cajun seasoning blend (salt-free)	Spice Islands
Chili sauce	Heinz
Chipotle chile powder	McCormick
Cocktail sauce	Heinz
Dry (ground) mustard	McCormick
Enchilada sauce	Las Palmas, La Victoria
Fish sauce	A Taste of Thai, Thai Kitchen

Hoisin sauce	Premier Japan
Hot pepper sauce	Tabasco, Frank's RedHot
Lemon pepper	McCormick, Durkee, Spice Islands
Mango chutney	Crosse & Blackwell Major Grey, Stonewall Kitchen, Silver Palate
Marinara sauce	Classico, Prego
Marinated artichokes	Mezzetta
Mediterranean herb seasoning	McCormick, Lawry's
Mexican salsa	Mission, Tostitos, Newman's Own, La Victoria, Pace
Mexican salsa verde	La Victoria
Montreal steak seasoning	McCormick Grill Mates
Pizza sauce	Classico, Prego
Salad dressing	Miracle Whip, Hy-Vee Lite
Seafood seasoning	Spice Islands, Old Bay
Seasoned salt	Lawry's
Soft silken tofu	Mori-Nu
Southwestern seasoning	McCormick Perfect Pinch Southwestern
Soy sauce (gluten-free tamari)	San-J, Kikkoman
Thai green curry paste	A Taste of Thai
Teriyaki sauce	Premier Japan, Kikkoman
Worcestershire sauce	French's (and Lea & Perrins in the U.S., not in Canada)
Tofu (soft, silken)	Mori-Nu

Dairy and Cheese

Buttery spread	Earth Balance
Cheese alternative	Vegan Gourmet, Daiya
Cream cheese alternative	Tofutti, Vegan Gourmet
Dry milk powder	Organic Valley
Dry milk powder substitute	Better Than Milk soy powder
Ice cream	Ben & Jerry's, Häagen-Dazs
Mozzarella or cheddar cheese alternative wedges	Vegan Gourmet, Daiya
Parmesan cheese	Galaxy
Provolone cheese	Daiya Swiss-style slices
Sour cream alternative	Tofutti, Vegan Gourmet
Soy milk	Silk
Soy Parmesan	Galaxy
Soy yogurt	WholeSoy
Whipped cream or whipped topping	Lucerne, Soyatoo

Flours and Grains

Almond meal/flour	Bob's Red Mill, Honeyville Farms
Amaranth (flour and whole grain)	Bob's Red Mill
Brown rice	Bob's Red Mill
Buckwheat flour	Bob's Red Mill (or grind Bob's Red Mill Creamy Buckwheat Hot Cereal into flour with a small coffee grinder)
Chickpea (garbanzo) flour	Bob's Red Mill
Garbanzo/fava bean flour	Bob's Red Mill
Corn grits (polenta)	Bob's Red Mill
Cornmeal (yellow)	Bob's Red Mill
Millet (flour and whole grain)	Bob's Red Mill
Oat bran	Bob's Red Mill
Oats (steel-cut)	Bob's Red Mill
Quinoa	Bob's Red Mill
Rice bran	Bob's Red Mill
Sorghum (flour and whole grain)	Bob's Red Mill, Shiloh Farms
Sweet rice flour	Bob's Red Mill
Teff	Bob's Red Mill, The Teff Company
Wild rice	Lundberg

Meats

Andouille sausage	Boar's Head
Deli meat	Boar's Head
Italian sausage	Applegate
Pepperoni slices	Hormel
Pork sausage	Applegate Farms

Pasta

Penne	Tinkyada, Dr. Schär
Linguine	Tinkyada
Spaghetti	Tinkyada

Soups

Beef broth	Swanson
Bouillon powder or cubes	Ener-G, Herb-Ox, Lee Kum Kee
Chicken broth	Swanson Natural Goodness
Vegetable broth	Imagine no-chicken (for its light color)

Vegetables (Canned)

Mexican-style tomatoes	Ro-Tel

Menus

Wondering how to organize the recipes in this cookbook into menus? Here are several ideas for both every day and special occasions. Although the whole menus may take longer than 30 minutes to prepare, you can certainly have these meals on the table quickly if you coordinate your work. For example, in the Weekend Light Lunch, make the Banana Bread Muffins batter first and then bake the muffins while you make the rest of the meal. Prepare and refrigerate the fruit cups, then begin the Quick and Easy Hash so that it's ready just as the muffins are done.

Weekend Brunch

Easy Pasta Frittata
Cranberry-Orange Scones with Orange Glaze
fresh fruit

Weekend Light Lunch

Quick and Easy Hash
Banana Bread Muffins
fruit cups

Spring Luncheon

Pesto Penne
steamed asparagus
French Baguettes
Berries in Gelatin

All-American Supper

Chicken-Fried Steak
mashed potatoes
steamed vegetables
Apple Crisp with Granola

Southwestern Meal

Mexican Skillet Beef and Rice
Spicy Black Beans
Guacamole
No-Cook Chocolate Cheesecakes

Southern Influence

Kale Salad
Shrimp and Grits
Corn Bread
Vanilla Cupcakes

Italian Dinner

Linguine with Red Clam Sauce
Focaccia Flatbread
mixed green salad
White Chocolate, Apricot, and Almond Balls

Asian Style

Grilled Grouper with Ginger-Orange Glaze
Coconut Rice
fruit sorbet

For Kids of All Ages

Mediterranean Pizza
fresh vegetables
Chocolate Brownies

Vegetarian Supper

Split Pea Dal with Rice
cooked greens
Corn Bread
Flourless Chocolate Cupcakes

Paleo Diet Dinner

Grilled T-Bone Florentine
roasted root vegetables
Grilled Fruit

Elegant Dinner Party

Gazpacho
Salmon en Papillote
Coconut Rice
French Baguettes
Cherry Clafouti

Breakfasts and Breads

BREAKFAST
French Toast
Savory French Toast
Muesli
Eggs in a Nest
Easy Pasta Frittata
Quick and Easy Hash
Breakfast Pizza

QUICK BREADS
Basic Muffins
Banana Bread Muffins
Cranberry-Orange Scones with Orange Glaze
Corn Bread
Microwave Muffin in a Mug
Parmesan Shortbread
Farinata with Sage and Onion
Buttermilk Biscuits

YEAST BREADS
French Baguettes
Focaccia Flatbread
Garlic Breadsticks

French Toast

MAKES: 6 SLICES **PREPARATION TIME:** 2 MINUTES **FRYING TIME:** 6 TO 10 MINUTES

French toast is always a treat—and totally possible—even with limited time. Mix up the batter the night before so all you have to do is dip and fry the next morning. Any sandwich bread works, but my family really likes cinnamon-raisin bread. To avoid sogginess, dip the bread in the batter just long enough to completely coat both sides rather than letting it get thoroughly soaked.

- 6 large eggs
- 2 cups milk of choice
- 2 tablespoons sugar
- 2 teaspoons pure vanilla extract
- ½ teaspoon ground cinnamon
- ¼ teaspoon freshly grated nutmeg
- ½ teaspoon salt
- 3 teaspoons butter or buttery spread, for frying
- 6 slices gluten-free sandwich bread
  Maple syrup or your favorite topping

1. In a large bowl, combine the eggs, milk, sugar, vanilla, cinnamon, nutmeg, and salt and whisk until blended.

2. In a large nonstick skillet (gray, not black), melt the butter over medium heat. Dip the slices of bread into the egg mixture just long enough to thoroughly coat both sides. Place the bread in the hot skillet, leaving 1 inch between slices.

3. Cook for 3 to 5 minutes per side, or until the toast is golden and crispy. Serve immediately, with maple syrup.

Storage: Leftovers can be refrigerated overnight, tightly wrapped in aluminum foil. To serve the next day, transfer to a baking sheet and bring to serving temperature in a preheated 300°F oven.

PER SLICE: 245 calories; 11g protein; 13g total fat; 1g fiber; 22g carbohydrates; 235mg cholesterol; 417mg sodium

Savory French Toast

MAKES: 4 SLICES   **PREPARATION TIME:** 2 MINUTES   **FRYING TIME:** 3 TO 5 MINUTES

French toast doesn't have to be sweet, as this savory version illustrates, and you could top it with a little marmalade or apple butter for a sweet contrast to the savory melted cheese. Or, use these as the base for a savory gravy or white sauce.

- 2 large eggs, beaten
- ½ cup milk of choice
- 1 cup shredded Monterey Jack cheese or cheese alternative
- 1 tablespoon chopped fresh chives (optional)
- 2 teaspoons butter or buttery spread
- 4 slices gluten-free sandwich bread
- ¼ cup grated Parmesan cheese or soy Parmesan
- ½ cup orange marmalade, apple butter, or fruit preserves of choice for topping (optional)

1. In a shallow bowl, whisk together the eggs, milk, cheese, and chives, if using. In a large nonstick skillet (gray, not black), melt the butter over medium heat. Dip the slices of bread into the egg mixture. (To avoid sogginess, dip the bread in the batter just long enough to thoroughly coat both sides rather than letting it soak.) Place the bread in the hot skillet, leaving 1 inch between slices.

2. Cook for 3 to 5 minutes per side, or until the toast is golden and crispy. Dust the tops with the Parmesan cheese. Serve hot with a small dollop of fruit preserves, if desired.

Storage: Leftovers can be refrigerated overnight, tightly wrapped in aluminum foil. To serve the next day, transfer to a baking sheet and bring to serving temperature in a preheated 300°F oven.

PER SLICE: 370 calories; 13g protein; 18g total fat; 3g fiber; 41g carbohydrates; 136mg cholesterol; 354mg sodium

Muesli

MAKES: 4 SERVINGS   PREPARATION TIME: 5 MINUTES   CHILLING TIME: OVERNIGHT
REHEATING TIME: 3 TO 5 MINUTES

This hearty breakfast dish can be kept in the refrigerator and served throughout the week. It is commonly served in European countries and is very creamy, hearty, and filling. Start with store-bought granola and it comes together in a flash.

3½ cups store-bought gluten-free granola*
2 apples (Gala or Fuji, or your choice), cored and diced
8 ounces plain low-fat yogurt or soy yogurt
1 cup milk of choice
1 tablespoon honey, or to taste
1 teaspoon pure vanilla extract

In a large bowl, toss all of the ingredients until well blended. Cover and refrigerate overnight or until the liquids are absorbed. Serve cold, or gently reheat in a microwave oven for 3 to 5 minutes, until warm.

Storage: *Refrigerate muesli in a bowl, tightly sealed, for up to 3 days. Serve cold, or gently reheat in the microwave for 3 to 5 minutes, until it reaches desired serving temperature.*

PER SERVING: 230 calories; 8g protein; 7g total fat; 4g fiber; 35g carbohydrates; 3mg cholesterol; 77mg sodium

* Check with your physician to make sure gluten-free oats are right for your diet.

Eggs in a Nest

MAKES: 4 SERVINGS   PREPARATION TIME: 5 MINUTES
BAKING TIME: 20 TO 25 MINUTES

This is a particularly good way to use up gluten-free bread that is hardened but not stale. Gently heat it on Low power in a microwave oven for 30 seconds or just until it is soft and pliable, and then proceed with this recipe. This dish is particularly good for weekends—for family or guests.

  4 slices gluten-free sandwich bread
  2 tablespoons chopped green onion
  2 tablespoons chopped fresh thyme
  4 large eggs
  ¼ teaspoon salt
  ¼ teaspoon freshly ground black pepper
  ¼ cup shredded Gruyère or Swiss cheese or cheese alternative
     Pinch of paprika, for garnish

1. Put a rack in the lowest position of the oven. Preheat the oven to 325°F. Generously grease four 6-ounce ramekins. Place the ramekins on a baking sheet (not nonstick).

2. Trim the crusts from the bread. With a rolling pin, flatten each slice of bread to a ⅛-inch thickness, and push and press the bread into the ramekin to line it.

3. Divide the green onion and half of the thyme evenly among the ramekins. Break an egg into each ramekin and season it with the salt and pepper. Top with the cheese and sprinkle with paprika.

4. Bake for 20 to 25 minutes or to your desired doneness for eggs. Remove from the oven and serve immediately, garnished with a sprinkle of the remaining thyme.

Storage: *Refrigerate leftovers, tightly covered, for up to 1 day.*

PER SERVING: 160 calories; 10g protein; 7g total fat; 1g fiber; 14g carbohydrates; 194mg cholesterol; 392mg sodium

Easy Pasta Frittata

MAKES: 4 SERVINGS   PREPARATION TIME: 5 MINUTES
FRYING TIME: 15 TO 20 MINUTES

Many people discard leftover pasta, but there are many flavorful ways to use it up. Any brand will work in this flavorful frittata, but I prefer Tinkyada linguine because it holds its shape so well. To save time, keep cleaned and chopped leeks in a tightly sealed plastic container in your freezer; they thaw quickly and save tons of time when preparing many dishes. Some frittatas are broiled in the oven during the final minutes; I don't do that here, but you can if you want a more browned top. Frittatas are perfect not only for breakfast but also for brunch, lunch, or dinner. For a vegetarian frittata, you can omit the prosciutto and add your favorite small or finely chopped veggies, such as peas or zucchini.

1 tablespoon canola oil

2 cups thinly sliced leeks (about 2), white section only, halved lengthwise and washed thoroughly

1 slice prosciutto or pancetta, finely chopped

4 large eggs

¼ cup milk of choice

¼ cup grated Parmesan cheese or soy Parmesan

½ teaspoon salt

¼ teaspoon freshly ground black pepper

2 teaspoons fresh oregano or 1 teaspoon dried

2 teaspoons fresh basil or 1 teaspoon dried

1½ cups (about 4 ounces) cooked gluten-free linguine

½ cup shredded low-fat mozzarella cheese or cheese alternative

2 tablespoons fresh parsley or 1 tablespoon dried

1. In a 10-inch nonstick skillet (gray, not black), heat 2 teaspoons of the canola oil over medium-low heat. Add the leeks and prosciutto and cook until the leeks are softened, about 4 minutes. Remove the skillet from the heat.

2. In a medium bowl, whisk together the eggs, milk, Parmesan cheese, salt, pepper, oregano, and basil. Stir in the cooked linguine.

3. Return the skillet to medium heat. Add the remaining 1 teaspoon canola oil. Pour the egg mixture into the pan, cover, and cook for 10 minutes or until the top is set. Remove the cover, sprinkle with the mozzarella cheese, and cover again. Cook for another 1 to 2 minutes, until the cheese is melted and the eggs are cooked through. Sprinkle with the parsley and serve immediately.

Storage: *Refrigerate leftovers overnight, tightly wrapped in plastic wrap. Before serving, bring to room temperature. The frittata can also be cut into small squares and served as appetizers.*

PER SERVING: 380 calories; 31g protein; 17g total fat; 2g fiber; 23g carbohydrates; 239mg cholesterol; 533mg sodium

HOW TO CLEAN LEEKS

Leeks, cousins of scallions and onions, lend marvelous flavor to food, but before adding them to any dish, they must be thoroughly washed to remove any dirt trapped between their layers. To clean them, slice off the dark green ends (too tough to eat) and the root end. Slice the leek in half lengthwise and separate the long layers. Then swish the leeks in a large bowl of water to dislodge the dirt. Lift the cleaned leeks out of the water with a slotted spoon so that the dirt is left behind in the bowl. If the leeks are very dirty, you may need to clean them in several changes of water.

Quick and Easy Hash

MAKES: 4 SERVINGS   PREPARATION TIME: 5 MINUTES
FRYING TIME: 25 TO 30 MINUTES

Hash is meant to use up leftovers, and it makes a hearty breakfast. Don't let this seemingly long list of ingredients intimidate you; it's all leftovers so they're already cooked. Once you make a hash, you'll see that there are no hard and fast rules—vary the ingredients based on what you have available at the time. I like eggs on my hash, but you can omit them if you wish.

- 3 tablespoons olive oil
- 2 cups leftover mashed potatoes (or cooked diced potatoes or hash browns)
- 1 cup chopped or shredded cooked turkey (or chicken, ham, or beef)
- ¼ cup gluten-free chicken broth
- 1 tablespoon gluten-free Worcestershire sauce
- 1 tablespoon Dijon mustard
- 2 tablespoons finely diced onion or 2 teaspoons dried minced onion
- ½ teaspoon celery salt
- ½ teaspoon freshly ground black pepper, plus more to taste
- 4 large eggs
- Paprika, for garnish
- 2 tablespoons chopped fresh parsley or 1 tablespoon dried

1. In a heavy, cast-iron skillet, heat 2 tablespoons of the olive oil over medium heat. Place the potatoes and meat in the skillet and cook, stirring, until heated through, about 10 minutes.

2. While the mixture heats, in a medium bowl, whisk together the broth, Worcestershire sauce, mustard, onion, celery salt, and pepper, and pour over the potatoes and meat.

3. With a spatula, press the mixture firmly down to compress it so all parts touch the skillet, and cook until deeply browned and crispy on the bottom. Flip the hash, add the remaining 1 tablespoon olive oil to the skillet, and cook the other side until deeply browned and crisp. Cooking time varies with the type of ingredients and their moisture content, so keep checking the browning process; when browner (but not burned), the better for crispiness and flavor.

4. Transfer the hash to a serving plate and cover with aluminum foil to keep warm.

5. Add the eggs to the same skillet and cook to the desired degree of doneness; season with salt and pepper to taste. Place the eggs on top of the hash, dust with paprika, and sprinkle with the parsley. Cut into wedges and serve immediately.

Storage: *Refrigerate leftovers, tightly covered, for up to 1 day.*

PER SERVING: 310 calories; 19g protein; 19g total fat; 2g fiber; 6g carbohydrates; 216mg cholesterol; 610mg sodium

USING LEFTOVERS SAVES TIME

Some dishes—such as hash—are perfect for using up leftovers. For the time-pressed cook, making a dish from leftovers is ideal because the ingredients are already cooked. Simply mix together with a few extra seasonings and then reheat to create a whole new dish with minimal effort and no waste. I often make a hash with leftovers from large holiday meals such as Thanksgiving turkey or Easter ham. However, even a simple steak and potatoes dinner can provide the base for a delicious steak hash. Use your imagination to create your own unique hash by adding leftover cooked vegetables or varying the seasonings as you wish.

Breakfast Pizza

MAKES: 6 SERVINGS   PREPARATION TIME: 10 MINUTES
BAKING TIME: PAR-BAKING = 10 MINUTES; SECOND BAKING = 10 TO 15 MINUTES

Some people secretly eat leftover pizza for breakfast. This one is made expressly for breakfast—why not? Pizza is so satisfying, and here, you get all the meat-and-egg flavors of a typical hearty breakfast. Save time by using cooked bacon, a store-bought or par-baked crust (see below), and mixing up the egg topping the night before. Or assemble and bake the entire pizza the day before, cut into slices, and refrigerate. Reheat slices on Low power in the microwave the next morning as needed.

- 1 (12-inch) store-bought gluten-free pizza crust (or par-baked homemade Pizza Crust, page 157)
- ½ cup store-bought gluten-free pizza sauce or homemade Basil Pizza Sauce (page 157)
- 4 bacon slices, cooked and diced, or 2 ounces pork sausage, browned
- 3 large eggs
- 1 tablespoon finely diced onion or 1 teaspoon dried minced onion
- ¼ teaspoon salt
- ⅛ teaspoon freshly ground black pepper
- ¾ cup shredded cheddar or Monterey Jack cheese or cheese alternative
- 2 tablespoons grated Parmesan cheese or soy Parmesan
  Thinly sliced green onions (green part only), for garnish

1. Place a rack in the middle of the oven. Preheat the oven to 400°F. Place the pizza crust on a 12-inch nonstick pizza pan (gray, not black). Brush evenly with the pizza sauce and sprinkle with the bacon. In a medium bowl, whisk together the eggs, onion, salt, and pepper until smooth, then pour evenly over the crust. Scatter the cheddar cheese evenly on top and sprinkle with the Parmesan cheese.

2. Bake until the eggs are set and the cheese is melted, 10 to 12 minutes. Remove from the oven, sprinkle with green onions, cool for 2 to 3 minutes, cut into 6 slices, and serve immediately.

Storage: Refrigerate leftovers, loosely wrapped in aluminum foil, overnight. Eat cold the next day or reheat slices on a baking sheet in a 300°F oven to the desired serving temperature.

PER SERVING: 300 calories; 11g protein; 15g total fat; 3g fiber; 33g carbohydrates; 114mg cholesterol; 750mg sodium

CONTINUED ON PAGE 34

CONTINUED FROM PAGE 33

IDEAS FOR QUICKER PIZZA

Pizza (especially gluten-free pizza) takes time to bake, since the soft dough works best with two bakings rather than one. To save precious time, par-bake one (or several) pizza crust(s) on the bottom rack of the oven for 15 minutes (or until lightly browned and crisp). Cool thoroughly, wrap tightly in aluminum foil or plastic wrap, and freeze for 1 month or refrigerate for 2 to 3 days. When you're ready to make pizza, place the crust on a 12-inch nonstick pizza pan (gray, not black), add the toppings, and bake on the middle rack of the oven as directed in the recipe.

QUICK BREADS

✺ Basic Muffins

MAKES: 12 MUFFINS   PREPARATION TIME: 5 MINUTES
BAKING TIME: 25 TO 30 MINUTES

These simple muffins are plain, but sometimes that's exactly what you want. And they make the perfect base for a huge variety of flavors.

     2 large eggs, at room temperature
    ¾ cup milk of choice, at room temperature
    ½ cup canola oil
     1 tablespoon grated lemon zest
     1 teaspoon pure vanilla extract
    2¼ cups Carol's Sorghum Blend (page 15)
    ¾ cup sugar
     1 tablespoon baking powder
    1½ teaspoons xanthan gum
    ¾ teaspoon salt

1. Place a rack in the middle of the oven. Preheat the oven to 375°F. Generously grease the cups of a 12-cup nonstick standard muffin pan (gray, not black) or line with paper liners.

2. In a medium mixing bowl, beat the eggs with an electric mixer on low speed until light yellow and frothy, about 30 seconds. Add the milk, oil, lemon zest, and vanilla and beat until just blended.

3. In a small bowl, whisk together the sorghum blend, sugar, baking powder, xanthan gum, and salt. With the mixer on low speed, gradually beat the dry ingredients into the liquid ingredients until the batter is smooth and just slightly thickened. Divide the batter evenly in the muffin cups.

4. Bake for 25 to 30 minutes or until the muffin tops are firm and the edges start to pull away from the pan. Cool the muffins in the pan for 10 minutes. Transfer the muffins to a wire rack to cool for another 5 minutes. Serve warm.

CONTINUED ON PAGE 36

CONTINUED FROM PAGE 35

Storage: *Store the muffins in a plastic storage bag at room temperature for up to 2 days, then refrigerate for up to another 2 days. Freeze in plastic storage bags for up to 1 month. Thaw at room temperature and reheat on Low power in the microwave in 10-second increments.*

PER MUFFIN: 235 calories; 3g protein; 10g total fat; 1g fiber; 35g carbohydrates; 32mg cholesterol; 272mg sodium

EASY WAYS TO VARY MUFFINS

Feel free to modify the recipe to suit your taste: Replace lemon zest with orange zest; or add a teaspoon of your favorite extract; or add ½ cup of any of the following after mixing the batter: chopped fresh fruit, chopped nuts, coconut flakes, finely chopped dried fruit, or chocolate chips. To add fiber, nutrients, and nutty flavor, add ¼ cup flax meal (ground flax), hemp, or chia seeds.

Banana Bread Muffins

MAKES: 12 MUFFINS   PREPARATION TIME: 10 MINUTES
BAKING TIME: 25 TO 30 MINUTES

Banana bread evokes fond memories of childhood, home, and family. So, save those extra-ripe bananas for this quintessential comfort-food favorite, but bake muffins to save time. Vary it by adding chocolate chips and different kinds of nuts; replace the raisins with dried cherries, cranberries, or currants. Or add ¼ cup of chia seeds, or ground flax or hemp seeds, to the batter for added nutrients and flavor. (Experiment until you find the flavor combination that you like.)

- 2 large eggs, at room temperature
- ⅓ cup canola oil
- 1 cup milk of choice, at room temperature
- 1 teaspoon pure vanilla extract
- 2 mashed ripe medium bananas (about 1 cup)
- 2⅓ cups Carol's Sorghum Blend (page 15)
- ¾ cup packed brown sugar
- 1½ teaspoons xanthan gum
- 2 teaspoons baking powder
- 1 teaspoon ground cinnamon
- 1 teaspoon salt
- ¼ teaspoon baking soda
- ½ cup chopped walnuts
- ½ cup dark raisins

1. Place a rack in the lower third of the oven. Preheat the oven to 375°F. Generously grease the cups of a 12-cup nonstick standard muffin pan (gray, not black) or line with paper liners.

2. In a large mixing bowl, beat the eggs, oil, milk, vanilla, and bananas with an electric mixer on low speed until thoroughly blended. In a medium bowl, whisk together the sorghum blend, brown sugar, xanthan gum, baking powder, cinnamon, salt, and baking soda until well blended. With the mixer on low speed, gradually beat the flour mixture into the egg mixture until just blended. Increase the speed to medium-low and beat until the batter slightly thickens, about 30 seconds. Stir in the nuts and raisins. Divide the batter evenly in the muffin cups.

CONTINUED ON PAGE 38

CONTINUED FROM PAGE 37

3. Bake until the tops are nicely browned and a toothpick inserted into the center comes out clean, 25 to 30 minutes. Cool the muffins in the pan for 10 minutes. Transfer the muffins to a wire rack to cool for another 5 minutes. Serve warm.

Storage: Store the muffins in a plastic storage bag at room temperature for up to 2 days, then refrigerate for up to another 2 days. Freeze in plastic storage bags for up to 1 month. Thaw at room temperature and reheat on Low power in the microwave in 10-second increments.

PER MUFFIN: 285 calories; 4g protein; 10g total fat; 2g fiber; 47g carbohydrates; 32mg cholesterol; 267mg sodium

38 100 BEST QUICK GLUTEN-FREE RECIPES

Cranberry-Orange Scones with Orange Glaze

MAKES: 8 SCONES   PREPARATION TIME: 5 MINUTES
BAKING TIME: 25 TO 30 MINUTES

Scones may sound fancy or complicated because they're often served with proper English tea, but they are actually quite rustic and incredibly easy. They are perfect for a weekend breakfast.

    1/3 cup butter or buttery spread, at room temperature
      1 large egg, at room temperature
    1/3 cup sugar
      1 tablespoon grated orange zest
    1/2 cup milk of choice, at room temperature
  11/2 cups Carol's Sorghum Blend (page 15)
    1/2 cup tapioca flour
      1 tablespoon baking powder
  11/2 teaspoons xanthan gum
      1 teaspoon guar gum
      1 teaspoon salt
    3/4 cup sweetened dried cranberries
      2 tablespoons cream or milk of choice, for brushing
      1 tablespoon sparkling sugar (or regular sugar), for sprinkling

ORANGE GLAZE

      2 tablespoons orange juice, or enough to make a thin glaze
      1 cup powdered sugar

1. Place a rack in the middle of the oven. Preheat the oven to 375°F. Generously grease a 9×13-inch nonstick baking sheet (gray, not black) or line it with parchment paper.

2. In a food processor, process the butter, egg, sugar, and orange zest until blended. Add the milk, sorghum blend, tapioca flour, baking powder, xanthan gum, guar gum, and salt, and process just until blended. Add the cranberries and pulse just until the cranberries are incorporated into the dough. The dough will seem too soft for shaping, but don't worry.

3. Place the dough on the baking sheet, patting it with a wet spatula into a smooth, uniform 8-inch circle that is 3/4 inch thick. Use the wet spatula to shape straight sides (rather than rounded) for more even browning. Brush the dough with the cream and sprinkle with the sparkling sugar.

CONTINUED ON PAGE 40

CONTINUED FROM PAGE 39

4. Bake for 20 minutes or until the dough is lightly browned. Remove the baking sheet from the oven and, using a sharp knife, cut the circle of dough into 8 wedges. Pull the wedges away from the center so they are at least 1 inch from each other and return to the oven for another 5 to 7 minutes of baking. This makes all edges of the scones crisp, rather than just the tops. Cool the scones for 5 minutes on the pan on a wire rack.

5. MAKE THE GLAZE: In a small bowl, stir the orange juice into the powdered sugar until smooth. With a pastry brush, brush the glaze onto the warm scones. Serve immediately.

Storage: Store the scones in a plastic storage bag at room temperature for up to 2 days, then refrigerate for up to another 2 days. Freeze in plastic storage bags for up to 1 month. Thaw at room temperature and reheat on Low power in the microwave in 10-second increments.

PER SCONE: 305 calories; 3g protein; 10g total fat; 2g fiber; 55g carbohydrates; 48mg cholesterol; 467mg sodium

Corn Bread

MAKES: 12 SERVINGS PREPARATION TIME: 10 MINUTES
BAKING TIME: 25 TO 30 MINUTES

Corn bread is the all-American quick bread and so easy to prepare. It bakes quickly, so it is a great choice to accompany dinner. Put it in the oven first and prepare the rest of the meal while it bakes. For a lighter texture, sift the dry ingredients together after measuring. I was raised in the Midwest, so my corn bread is more cake-like and sweeter than the Southern version. We eat it with the meal as a savory side, then drizzle another piece with honey for dessert.

1¼ cups cornmeal
1 cup Carol's Sorghum Blend (page 15)
⅓ cup sugar
2 teaspoons baking powder
1 teaspoon xanthan gum
1 teaspoon salt
⅛ teaspoon baking soda
2 large eggs, at room temperature
1 cup water, at room temperature
⅓ cup canola oil

1. Place a rack in the lower third of the oven. Preheat the oven to 350°F. Generously grease an 8-inch round or square nonstick baking pan (gray, not black).

2. In a large mixing bowl, whisk together the cornmeal, sorghum blend, sugar, baking powder, xanthan gum, salt, and baking soda until well blended. With an electric mixer on low speed, beat in the eggs, water, and oil just until blended. Increase the speed to medium-low and beat until the batter is slightly thickened, about 30 seconds. The batter will be the consistency of thick cake batter. Spread the batter evenly in the pan.

3. Bake until the top is firm and a toothpick inserted into the center comes out clean, 25 to 30 minutes. Cool the corn bread in the pan on a wire rack for 10 minutes. Cut into 12 pieces and serve warm.

Storage: *Store corn bread, tightly wrapped, in the baking pan at room temperature for up to 2 days, then refrigerate in the pan, tightly covered, for up to another 2 days. Freeze leftovers wrapped in aluminum foil for up to 1 month. Thaw at room temperature and reheat slices on very low power in the microwave in 10-second increments to reach desired serving temperature.*

PER SERVING: 175 calories; 3g protein; 7g total fat; 2g fiber; 26g carbohydrates; 31mg cholesterol; 282mg sodium

Microwave Muffin in a Mug

MAKES: 4 SERVINGS   PREPARATION TIME: 10 MINUTES
COOKING TIME: 60 TO 70 SECONDS

Use this muffin recipe when you're pressed for time. Although you could make the muffins from start to finish quickly right when you need them, here's the most efficient way: Whisk together the dry ingredients the night before and put them in a covered bowl on the countertop. In a separate bowl, whisk together the egg, molasses, and oil until smooth and then refrigerate, tightly covered. Next morning, grease the mugs, then whisk together the dry and wet ingredients, and divide the batter evenly among the mugs. Cook in the microwave, and in a minute you will have fresh, hot, über-healthy muffins. Eat them immediately right out of the mug! Easy!

1 cup ground flax meal
2 tablespoons chopped walnuts
1 teaspoon baking powder
1/2 teaspoon apple pie spice or pumpkin pie spice
1/4 teaspoon salt
1 large egg
1/4 cup molasses (not blackstrap)
2 tablespoons canola oil

1. Grease 4 shallow, microwave-safe coffee mugs (the size of the mugs will determine how high the muffins will rise and how quickly they will cook). In a small bowl, whisk together the flax meal, walnuts, baking powder, apple pie spice, and salt until well blended. Add the egg, molasses, and oil, and whisk until thoroughly blended. The batter will be droopy-soft. Divide the batter among the mugs. Place the mugs on saucers or plates to catch any drips.

2. Microwave on High power for 60 to 70 seconds. The muffins will rise up and possibly fall over the side of the mug (depending on the mug size). The muffins are done when they are no longer shiny; cooking time may vary depending on the wattage of your microwave oven. (They won't brown like muffins baked in a regular oven.) Remove from the microwave and cool slightly before eating right out of the mug. Or run a sharp knife around the edge to loosen and remove the muffin from the mug. Serve immediately.

CONTINUED ON PAGE 44

CONTINUED FROM PAGE 43

Storage: *These muffins are best eaten immediately after cooking.*

PER SERVING: 345 calories; 10g protein; 23g total fat; 11g fiber; 28g carbohydrates; 47mg cholesterol; 290mg sodium

HEALTHY OPTIONS FOR MUG MUFFINS

These muffins are very versatile. Instead of flax meal, use gluten-free oat flour. Rather than molasses, use maple syrup. Replace the apple pie spice with ground cinnamon. Use melted coconut oil rather than canola oil. The possibilities are endless, and finished taste and texture will vary depending on your modifications, but this allows you to tailor this muffin recipe to suit your needs.

Parmesan Shortbread

MAKES: 8 SERVINGS **PREPARATION TIME:** 5 MINUTES
BAKING TIME: 30 TO 35 MINUTES

This thick cracker-like bread can be eaten with soups and stews and is a nice crispy accompaniment to a smooth, creamy soup. For convenience, you can use pre-grated Parmesan cheese that comes in tubs, but if you want to grate the Parmesan cheese yourself, start with a 1-ounce chunk.

- ½ cup (1 stick) butter or buttery spread
- 2 tablespoons sugar
- 2 cups Carol's Sorghum Blend (page 15)
- ¼ cup cornstarch
- ½ teaspoon xanthan gum
- ½ teaspoon salt
- ½ cup milk of choice
- ⅓ cup grated Parmesan cheese or soy Parmesan (about 1 ounce)
- ¼ teaspoon butter-flavored salt or regular salt

1. Place a rack in the middle of the oven. Preheat the oven to 350°F. Line a 9×13-inch nonstick rimmed baking sheet (gray, not black) with parchment paper.

2. In a food processor, process the butter and sugar until well blended. Add the sorghum blend, cornstarch, xanthan gum, and salt and pulse a few times to blend. Add the milk and Parmesan cheese and process until the mixture forms a ball, stopping to scrape down the side of the bowl if necessary. The dough will be somewhat stiff and feel firm rather than soft and sticky.

3. Place the dough in the center of the parchment paper and roll or pat into an 8-inch circle, ½ inch thick. Flute the outer edges of the circle decoratively with your fingers and prick the center of the circle a few times with a fork. Cut the dough into 8 wedges and sprinkle with the butter-flavored salt.

4. Bake for 30 to 35 minutes, until the edges are golden brown. Cool the shortbread on the pan on a wire rack for 10 minutes. Serve warm or at room temperature.

Storage: *Store leftovers, tightly wrapped, at room temperature for up to 2 days.*

PER SERVING: 265 calories; 4g protein; 13g total fat; 1g fiber; 36g carbohydrates; 34mg cholesterol; 272mg sodium

Farinata with Sage and Onion

MAKES: 4 SERVINGS   PREPARATION TIME: 2 MINUTES
STANDING TIME: 1 HOUR TO OVERNIGHT   BAKING TIME: 12 TO 15 MINUTES

Farinata is a thin, pizza-like Italian pancake made from chickpea (garbanzo) flour and served as bread. It varies depending on where it is made, and it is known as socca in France. When I first tried this bread, it was so good that I ate the whole batch myself. So be prepared—you or your family may like it so much that you might have to make several batches. Farinata can be made in a regular cast-iron skillet, but it won't be quite as crisp or easy to remove because of the skillet's straight—rather than sloping—sides. The batter requires a standing time of at least an hour before baking; you can do other things in the meantime, and it's worth the wait.

    1 cup chickpea flour or garbanzo flour
    1 tablespoon finely diced onion or 1 teaspoon dried minced onion
 ¾ teaspoon salt
 ½ teaspoon freshly ground black pepper
    1 tablespoon chopped fresh sage or rosemary
    1 cup lukewarm (100°F) water
    5 tablespoons olive oil
      Coarse salt, for sprinkling

1. In a small bowl, whisk together the flour, onion, salt, pepper, and sage. Slowly whisk in the water until no lumps remain. Stir in 3 tablespoons of the olive oil. Cover and let stand at room temperature, tightly covered, for at least 1 hour or up to overnight.

2. Place a rack in the middle of the oven. Preheat the oven to 450°F. While the oven preheats, place a 10-inch cast-iron round flat griddle or skillet with at least a ⅜-inch rim into the oven to heat it. When the batter is ready, remove the griddle with an oven mitt. Pour the remaining 2 tablespoons of oil into the griddle, tilting it to evenly coat the bottom. Pour the batter into the griddle, swirling to cover the pan evenly.

3. Bake for 12 to 15 minutes, until the farinata is firm to the touch. For deeper browning, set the farinata, still in the griddle, about 6 inches from the broiler and broil just long enough to lightly brown the top. Sprinkle with coarse salt, cut into wedges, and serve immediately.

Storage: Farinata is best eaten immediately after baking.

PER SERVING: 235 calories; 5g protein; 18g total fat; 3g fiber; 14g carbohydrates; 0mg cholesterol; 417mg sodium

Buttermilk Biscuits

MAKES: 10 BISCUITS   PREPARATION TIME: 10 MINUTES
BAKING TIME: 12 TO 15 MINUTES

Don't be puzzled by this ultrasoft biscuit dough—this texture is necessary for proper rising. When dusted with rice flour, it becomes manageable. Serve these biscuits with honey, jam, or jelly. For strawberry shortcake biscuits, add ½ cup sugar and bake as directed. For deeper browning of the biscuits, whisk an egg yolk into the 2 tablespoons of milk before brushing the tops.

Brown rice flour, for dusting and rolling
¾ cup Carol's Sorghum Blend (page 15)
¾ cup potato starch
4 teaspoons sugar
1 tablespoon baking powder
1 teaspoon xanthan gum
1 teaspoon guar gum
½ teaspoon baking soda
½ teaspoon salt
¼ cup shortening
1 cup buttermilk, well shaken, or homemade buttermilk (page 123), or plain kefir or cultured coconut milk, at room temperature
2 tablespoons milk of choice or cream

1. Place a rack in the middle of the oven. Preheat the oven to 375°F. Line two 9×13-inch nonstick baking sheets (gray, not black) with parchment paper. Place a large sheet of parchment paper on the countertop and dust lightly with rice flour.

2. In a food processor, pulse the sorghum blend, potato starch, sugar, baking powder, xanthan gum, guar gum, baking soda, and salt to mix thoroughly. Add the shortening and buttermilk and process until the dough forms a ball, scraping down the side with a spatula, if necessary. The dough will be very, very soft.

3. Place the dough on the parchment paper. Lightly dust it with rice flour to facilitate easier handling. Gently pat the dough to a 1-inch-thick circle on the parchment paper. Cut into 8 biscuits, 2 inches in diameter, with a floured biscuit cutter. For better rising, push the biscuit cutter straight down on the dough rather than twisting it while cutting. Remove the uncut dough and lift the cut biscuits onto

CONTINUED ON PAGE 50

CONTINUED FROM PAGE 49

the baking sheet, parchment paper and all. On a second sheet of dusted parchment paper, shape the remaining dough into a 1-inch-thick round and cut again. Lift the cut biscuits and parchment paper onto the second baking sheet and gently brush all of the biscuit tops with the milk.

4. Bake for 12 to 15 minutes, until the biscuits are nicely browned and crisp. Serve immediately.

Storage: *Store cooled biscuits in a plastic storage bag at room temperature for up to 1 day. Freeze in a plastic storage bag for up to 1 month. Reheat on very low power in the microwave in 5-second increments.*

PER BISCUIT: 135 calories; 1g protein; 5g total fat; 1g fiber; 22g carbohydrates; 1mg cholesterol; 343mg sodium

French Baguettes

MAKES: 3 BAGUETTES (TWENTY-ONE 1-INCH SERVINGS)
PREPARATION TIME: 10 MINUTES   **BAKING TIME:** 25 TO 30 MINUTES

A crispy crust makes this baguette a delight to eat, and it also makes a fantastic base for appetizers like bruschetta and crostini. It bakes quickly because I use a three-loaf French baguette pan and start baking it in a cold oven—an unusual but very effective method that makes perfect baguettes.

    1 tablespoon active dry yeast
    2 tablespoons sugar
    1 cup plus 2 tablespoons warm (110°F) water
    3 large egg whites (½ cup), at room temperature
    2 cups potato starch
    1 cup Carol's Sorghum Blend (page 15)
    1 teaspoon xanthan gum
    1 teaspoon guar gum
    1 teaspoon salt
    ¼ cup (½ stick) butter or buttery spread, or canola oil
    2 teaspoons cider vinegar
    1 tablespoon egg white whisked with 1 tablespoon water, for egg wash
    1 teaspoon sesame seeds

1. In a small bowl, dissolve the yeast and 1 teaspoon of the sugar in the warm water. Set aside to foam for 5 minutes.

2. Grease a French baguette pan (with three indentations) or line with parchment paper (necessary for perforated pans).

3. In the bowl of a heavy-duty stand mixer, combine the egg whites, potato starch, sorghum blend, xanthan gum, guar gum, salt, butter, and vinegar plus the remaining sugar and the yeast-water mixture. Beat on low speed to blend, and then beat on medium speed for 30 seconds, stirring down the side of the bowl with a spatula. The dough will be soft.

CONTINUED ON PAGE 52

CONTINUED FROM PAGE 51

4. Divide the dough among the indentations of the prepared pan. A #12 metal spring-action ice cream scoop helps ensure loaves of the same size. Smooth each third into a 9-inch log with a wet spatula, taking care to make each log the same length and thickness, with blunt rather than tapered ends. Brush with the egg wash. With a sharp knife, make three diagonal slashes ⅛ inch deep in each loaf so steam can escape during baking. Sprinkle with the sesame seeds.

5. Place immediately on the middle rack of a cold oven. Set the oven temperature to 425°F and bake for 25 to 30 minutes, until nicely browned. Cover the loaves with aluminum foil after 15 minutes of baking to prevent overbrowning.

6. Remove the bread from the pan and cool completely on a wire rack before slicing with a serrated knife or an electric knife.

Storage: Store whole baguettes at room temperature in plastic storage bags for up to 2 days. Then freeze the baguettes in bags for up to 1 month; thaw the bread in the bags at room temperature. To serve, remove from the bag and reheat slices in the microwave on Low power in 3- to 5-second increments until slightly warm. You can skip the rewarming if you are using the slices as the base for bruschetta or crostini.

PER SERVING: 95 calories; 1g protein; 1g total fat; 2g fiber; 19g carbohydrates; 6mg cholesterol; 110mg sodium

STARTING BREAD TO BAKE IN A COLD OVEN

It may seem unusual to start bread in a cold oven, especially when most of us have been taught to preheat the oven before baking anything. In reality, though, the cold-oven method works quite nicely with narrow or thin loaves like French Baguettes (or Garlic Breadsticks, page 56). It does not work well with standard loaf sizes because they are too thick for the oven heat to penetrate quickly enough to bake them properly.

Gluten-free bread dough is heavy and wet; as the oven preheats, it warms the wet dough and activates the yeast, causing the bread to rise quickly, but that's OK because the loaf is narrow, it doesn't have to rise as much as a standard 5×9-inch loaf, and the heat from the oven dries out the crust to make it crisp. It also means that a loaf of French bread spends only 30 to 35 minutes in the oven compared to nearly an hour for a regular loaf that requires rising time and then baking time. The bottom line? You will have bread much faster with the cold-oven method than with the preheated oven method. This method works perfectly in my KitchenAid wall oven, but it doesn't work in all ovens—especially those with quick preheat cycles. Try it once in your oven; if it doesn't work, then use the traditional method of first rising the dough and then baking it in a pre-heated 425°F oven for 25 to 30 minutes.

Focaccia Flatbread

MAKES: 10 SERVINGS   PREPARATION TIME: 10 MINUTES
BAKING TIME: 20 TO 25 MINUTES

Focaccia is a cross between flatbread and pizza. Here, it is spread in an ultrathin layer for a shorter baking time. Or, make the dough up to 2 days ahead and refrigerate until you're ready to bake—but be sure to use cold milk and eggs. This bread is delicious dipped in extra-virgin olive oil—just like they do in restaurants.

FLATBREAD

- 1½ teaspoons active dry yeast
- 2 teaspoons sugar
- ¾ cup warm (110°F) milk of choice
- 1½ cups Carol's Sorghum Blend (page 15)
- 1 teaspoon xanthan gum
- 1 teaspoon dried rosemary, crushed in your palm
- ¾ teaspoon salt
- ½ teaspoon onion powder
- 2 large eggs, at room temperature
- 2 tablespoons olive oil
- 2 teaspoons cider vinegar

TOPPING

- 1 tablespoon olive oil
- 1¼ teaspoons dried Italian seasoning
- ¼ teaspoon coarse sea salt
- 1 tablespoon grated Parmesan cheese or soy Parmesan

1. MAKE THE FLATBREAD: Dissolve the yeast and sugar in the warm milk. Set aside to foam for 5 minutes. Generously grease a 9×13-inch nonstick pan (gray, not black).

2. Whisk together the flour blend, xanthan gum, rosemary, salt, and onion powder in a large mixing bowl. Add the yeast-milk mixture, the eggs, olive oil, and vinegar and beat with an electric mixer on low speed until the dough thickens, about 1 minute. The dough will be soft and very sticky.

3. Transfer the dough to the pan and smooth the top with a wet spatula. Sprinkle with the topping ingredients: the olive oil, Italian seasoning, salt, and Parmesan cheese.

4. Place the pan on the middle rack of a cold oven. Turn the oven to 400°F. Bake for 20 to 25 minutes or until the top is golden brown and firm. To serve, cut into squares or tear into pieces while still slightly warm.

Storage: Store leftover flatbread at room temperature, tightly wrapped in aluminum foil, for up to 2 days. Then freeze in the foil for up to 1 month. Thaw at room temperature in the foil. If desired, reheat on Low power in the microwave in 10-second increments.

PER SERVING: 110 calories; 3g protein; 3g total fat; 1g fiber; 19g carbohydrates; 38mg cholesterol; 181mg sodium

FOCACCIA PIZZA

Focaccia is typically served as bread, but it also makes a perfect base for pizza. About 10 minutes before the focaccia is done baking, remove it from the oven, but leave it in the pan. Top with a thin layer of your favorite pizza fixings, such as pizza sauce, pepperoni, cheese, and cooked vegetables. Return the pan to the oven. The cheese will melt and the toppings will warm as the bread finishes baking. After removing the pizza from the oven, let it stand for 5 minutes, then cut into slices and serve.

Garlic Breadsticks

MAKES: 10 BREADSTICKS   **PREPARATION TIME:** 10 MINUTES
BAKING TIME: 15 TO 20 MINUTES

Breadsticks are especially fun with an Italian meal, and gluten-free guests will be particularly charmed that you would serve something they rarely get to eat. The cold-oven technique saves precious time. These breadsticks are deliciously bready and chewy rather than crisp and crunchy.

- 1 tablespoon active dry yeast
- ¾ cup warm (110°F) milk of choice
- ½ cup Carol's Sorghum Blend (page 15)
- ½ cup potato starch
- 1 tablespoon sugar
- 2 teaspoons xanthan gum
- 2 tablespoons grated Parmesan cheese or soy Parmesan
- ½ to ¾ teaspoon salt
- ½ teaspoon garlic powder
- 1 tablespoon olive oil
- 2 teaspoons cider vinegar
- 1 egg white, beaten to a foam, for egg wash (optional)
- 1 teaspoon sesame seeds (optional)

1. In a small bowl, dissolve the yeast in the warm milk. Set aside to foam for 5 minutes. Place an oven rack in the middle position in the oven. Generously grease a 10×15-inch baking sheet (not nonstick) or line with parchment paper.

2. In a medium mixer bowl, blend the yeast-milk mixture, sorghum blend, potato starch, sugar, xanthan gum, Parmesan cheese, salt, garlic powder, oil, and vinegar with an electric mixer on low speed just until smooth, about 30 seconds. Or, process the ingredients in a food processor until thoroughly combined. The dough will be soft and sticky.

3. Place the dough in a large, heavy-duty food-storage bag, squeeze out the air, and seal the bag. To form the breadsticks, cut a ½-inch opening diagonally on one corner; that will make a 1-inch circle in the bag for 1-inch-wide breadsticks.

CONTINUED ON PAGE 58

CONTINUED FROM PAGE 57

4. Squeeze the dough out of the plastic bag onto the sheet in 10 strips, each 1 inch wide by 6 inches long. For best results, hold the bag at a 90-degree angle to the baking sheet as you squeeze. Also, hold the bag with the seams perpendicular to the baking sheet, rather than horizontal, for a more authentic-looking breadstick. Brush the bread sticks with the egg white (if using) or lightly coat with cooking spray for a crispier, shinier breadstick. Sprinkle with the sesame seeds (if using).

5. Put the baking sheet on the middle rack of a cold oven and set the oven to 400°F. Bake for 15 to 20 minutes, until the breadsticks are golden brown. Rotate the baking sheet a quarter turn halfway through baking to ensure even browning. Cool the breadsticks for 5 minutes on the baking sheet. Serve slightly warm.

Storage: *Store the breadsticks at room temperature in a plastic storage bag for up to 1 day, then freeze in the bag for up to 1 month. Thaw the breadsticks in the bag at room temperature. To serve, gently reheat on Low power in the microwave in 3- to 5-second increments.*

PER BREADSTICK: 85 calories; 2g protein; 2g total fat; 1g fiber; 15g carbohydrates; 2mg cholesterol; 141mg sodium

Soups, Salads, Sandwiches, and Snacks

SOUPS
Gazpacho
Tuscan Bean Soup
Mediterranean Tomato Soup with Rice

SALADS
Kale Salad
Waldorf Salad
Orange-Olive Salad

SANDWICHES
Simple Cheese Quesadillas
Bean Quesadillas
Shrimp Tostadas with Chipotle Sauce
English Muffin Pepperoni Pizzas
Thai Chicken Salad Wraps
Sloppy Joes

SNACKS
Creamy White Bean Dip
Pinto Bean Dip
Crab Cocktail Spread
Stuffed Dates
Loaded Potato Skins
Brie with Honey and Chopped Nuts

✳ Gazpacho

MAKES: 4 SERVINGS (GENEROUS ¾ CUP EACH)   **PREPARATION TIME:** 15 MINUTES
CHILLING TIME: 1 HOUR TO OVERNIGHT

Gazpacho is traditionally made with fresh vegetables that require chopping, but this easy version uses canned diced tomatoes and store-bought salsa, plus a few fresh cucumbers and peppers to add crunch, all quickly chopped in a food processor. I also omitted the bread that usually thickens gazpacho because the texture is fine without it. The sweetness of the pineapple tempers the tomato's acidity. Gazpacho is often served as an appetizer in small cups or glassware rather than as a main dish. If you want larger servings, simply double the recipe and/or add small cooked shrimp, if you wish.

- 1 (14.5-ounce) can petite diced tomatoes, undrained
- 1 small yellow bell pepper, cored and cut in ½-inch slices
- 1 (4-inch) piece English (or hothouse) cucumber, unpeeled and cut into ½-inch slices
- 1 (8-ounce) can crushed pineapple in juice, undrained
- ¼ cup store-bought gluten-free Mexican salsa
- ¼ cup chopped fresh cilantro
- 2 teaspoons chopped onion or ½ teaspoon dried minced onion
- ½ teaspoon ground coriander
- ¼ teaspoon salt
- ¼ teaspoon freshly ground black pepper
- 1 tablespoon red wine vinegar
- 1 avocado, pitted, peeled, and chopped

1. In a food processor, combine half of the tomatoes along with the bell pepper and cucumber. Pulse until the bell pepper and cucumber are chopped finely.

2. Transfer the mixture to a large bowl and add the remaining tomatoes, the crushed pineapple, salsa, 3 tablespoons of the cilantro, the onion, coriander, salt, pepper, and vinegar. Refrigerate for at least 1 hour or overnight.

3. Divide evenly among four small cups, glasses, or bowls. Garnish with the avocado and remaining 1 tablespoon chopped fresh cilantro and serve immediately.

Storage: *Refrigerate ungarnished gazpacho in a glass bowl, tightly covered, for up to 2 days.*

PER SERVING: 165 calories; 4g protein; 8g total fat; 4g fiber; 24g carbohydrates; 1mg cholesterol; 224mg sodium

Tuscan Bean Soup

MAKES: 4 SERVINGS (ABOUT 1 CUP EACH)   PREPARATION TIME: 30 MINUTES

This simple yet flavorful bean soup is vegetarian when made with vegetable broth, but can be expanded to include bits of sausage, prosciutto, or pancetta (uncured Italian bacon), and vegetables such as onions, carrots, tomato, kale, Swiss chard, spinach, celery, potatoes, and/or cabbage, to make a hearty main dish. You can also add additional rosemary, fennel, or parsley for flavor. Serve it with your favorite gluten-free bread or crackers and perhaps a mixed green salad.

- 2 tablespoons olive oil
- 1 small onion, diced
- 1 carrot, peeled and cut into ⅛-inch slices
- 2 (15-ounce) cans navy beans, rinsed and drained
- 1 medium ripe tomato, chopped
- 2 tablespoons chopped fresh parsley, plus more for garnish
- 1 teaspoon dried sage, or to taste
- 1 teaspoon chopped fresh rosemary or ½ teaspoon crushed dried
- 1 tablespoon tomato paste
- 2 cups gluten-free low-sodium vegetable broth (or chicken broth)

In a heavy medium saucepan, heat the olive oil over medium heat. Cook the onion and carrot until soft, 5 to 7 minutes. Add all of the remaining ingredients and simmer, covered, for 20 to 25 minutes, or until the vegetables are tender. Add more broth or water if the soup appears dry. Serve hot, garnished with parsley.

Storage: *Refrigerate leftovers in a glass bowl, tightly covered, for up to 3 days.*

PER SERVING: 415 calories; 25g protein; 8g total fat; 13g fiber; 64g carbohydrates; 0mg cholesterol; 305mg sodium

Mediterranean Tomato Soup with Rice

MAKES: 4 SERVINGS (ABOUT 1 CUP EACH)   PREPARATION TIME: 25 MINUTES

Brimming with the flavors of southern France, this vegetarian soup thickens as the instant rice that's added cooks in the broth, instead of using the usual wheat flour as a thickener. A store-bought herb seasoning makes this recipe a snap to prepare. If you don't like tomato chunks in your soup, puree the tomatoes in a blender before you cook them. To make this a main dish, use chicken broth and add cooked shrimp or a leftover cooked white fish, such as cod or sole, just before serving.

- 2 (14.5-ounce) cans gluten-free low-sodium vegetable broth (or chicken broth)
- 1 (14.5-ounce) cans petite diced tomatoes, undrained
- ¼ cup diced onion or 1 tablespoon dried minced onion
- 2 teaspoons Mediterranean herb seasoning
- ½ teaspoon sugar
- ¼ teaspoon salt
- ¼ cup instant brown rice

Combine all of the ingredients in a 2-quart heavy saucepan. Bring to a boil over high heat, then reduce the heat to low and simmer, covered, for 20 minutes. Serve hot.

Storage: *Refrigerate leftovers in a glass bowl, tightly covered, for up to 2 days.*

PER SERVING: 100 calories; 11g protein; 1g total fat; 2g fiber; 15g carbohydrates; 0mg cholesterol; 572mg sodium

Kale Salad

MAKES: 4 SERVINGS PREPARATION TIME: 10 MINUTES

Kale, a popular cabbage, includes the flat-leaf types—often labeled as dinosaur, Tuscan, or lacinato—and the curly varieties. The flat-leaf types are easier to clean—or buy pre-shredded, ready-to-eat bags in the produce section. The mix of flavors in this dish is fascinating: green kale, fruity vinegar and apple, and salty Parmesan. Delicious and naturally gluten-free, this salad is an exciting, nutritious, hearty alternative to traditional mixed green salads.

- 6 cups shredded kale or 1 (5-ounce) bag shredded kale
- 2 tablespoons sherry vinegar (or fruit vinegar such as pear or raspberry)
- 2 tablespoons extra-virgin olive oil
- 1 teaspoon agave nectar or honey
- ⅛ teaspoon salt
- ⅛ teaspoon freshly ground black pepper
- 1 medium Honeycrisp apple, cored and cut into ⅛-inch slices
- ¼ cup walnuts, toasted and coarsely chopped (see page 98)
  Dusting of Parmesan cheese, for garnish (optional)

Place the kale in a large serving bowl. In a small bowl, whisk together the vinegar, oil, and agave nectar until smooth. Drizzle over the kale and toss until it is thoroughly coated. Add salt and pepper and let stand for 10 minutes to let the dressing slightly soften the kale. Add the apples and walnuts, toss again, dust with Parmesan cheese (if using), and serve.

Storage: *Refrigerate leftovers in a glass bowl, tightly covered, for up to 1 day. However, this salad is best eaten on the same day it is made.*

PER SERVING: 185 calories; 5g protein; 12g total fat; 3g fiber; 18g carbohydrates; 0mg cholesterol; 43mg sodium

Waldorf Salad

MAKES: 4 SERVINGS   PREPARATION TIME: 10 MINUTES

I make this naturally gluten-free salad at least once a week because
we love it so much. It is our standby salad because it incorporates
fruits, vegetables, and fiber into our diet in a flavorful way. It also
complements fish, poultry, or beef well.

  2 crisp red apples (Gala, Jonathan, or Honeycrisp)
  2 celery stalks, trimmed and cut into 1-inch diagonal slices
  ½ cup pecan or walnut pieces
  ¼ cup dried cranberries, dried cherries, dried currants, or dried dates
  1 tablespoon lemon juice
  1 tablespoon honey or agave nectar
  2 tablespoons Miracle Whip dressing or other gluten-free salad
    dressing spread
    Pinch of salt

1. Quarter and core the apples. Cut into ½-inch pieces and combine
with the celery, pecans, and cranberries in a medium serving bowl.

2. In a separate bowl, whisk together the lemon juice, honey, and
dressing until smooth. Pour over the apple mixture and toss to coat
thoroughly. Serve immediately, or refrigerate until serving time.

*Storage: Refrigerate leftovers in the serving bowl, tightly covered, for
up to 1 day. However, this salad is best eaten on the same day it is
made.*

PER SERVING: 200 calories; 1g protein; 15g total fat; 3g fiber; 18g carbohydrates;
2mg cholesterol; 57mg sodium

Orange-Olive Salad

MAKES: 6 SERVINGS   PREPARATION TIME: 5 MINUTES

This naturally gluten-free salad is gorgeous yet simple to create and lends important nutrients and incredible flavor and variety to a gluten-free diet. The salty olives balance the sweetness and tartness of the oranges. To keep it fresh and attractive, add the dressing just before serving. I serve this often during the winter, when oranges are at their best, but it is very pretty served in summer if you can get good oranges.

   3 navel oranges, peeled, seeded, and sliced into ¼-inch rounds
   1 red onion, thinly sliced
   ½ (16-ounce) jar drained pitted kalamata (or other seasoned black) olives, or to taste
   ½ teaspoon salt
   ½ teaspoon freshly ground black pepper
   2 tablespoons extra-virgin olive oil
   2 tablespoons red wine vinegar
   ¼ cup chopped fresh cilantro

1. In a large serving bowl, toss together the oranges, onion, olives, salt, and pepper.

2. Whisk the oil and vinegar together in a small jar. Pour over the orange mixture and toss gently to coat thoroughly. Sprinkle with the cilantro, and serve immediately.

Storage: Refrigerate leftovers in the serving bowl, tightly covered, for up to 1 day. Let stand at room temperature for 20 minutes before serving.

PER SERVING: 185 calories; 1g protein; 15g total fat; 2g fiber; 13g carbohydrates; 0mg cholesterol; 783mg sodium

✹ Simple Cheese Quesadillas

MAKES: 4 SERVINGS (½ QUESADILLA EACH)   PREPARATION TIME: 5 MINUTES
COOKING TIME: 15 MINUTES

Queso means "cheese" in Spanish; quesadillas are toasted Spanish cheese sandwiches made from tortillas instead of bread. They are perfect for children and adults alike. This version is vegetarian, but you can add meat—perhaps shredded chicken, beef, or pork. I prefer Rudi's gluten-free tortillas for this dish because they are very pliable and are available in three delicious flavors—plain, fiesta, and spinach.

CHEESE FILLING
   8 ounces cheddar cheese, shredded, or cheese alternative
   ¼ cup chopped fresh cilantro

TORTILLAS
   1 tablespoon canola oil
   4 Rudi's gluten-free flour tortillas

1. MAKE THE FILLING: Combine the cheese and cilantro in a small bowl. Set aside.

2. MAKE THE TORTILLAS: Brush half of the canola oil on a flat, nonstick grill pan or skillet (gray, not black) large enough to hold a tortilla. Gently lay a tortilla on the grill pan. Do not turn on the heat yet.

3. Spoon the cheese filling over the tortilla. With a spatula, gently spread the filling evenly over the tortilla to within ½ inch of the edge. Gently lay a second tortilla on top and gently press down.

4. Turn the heat to medium and cook, covered with a lid large enough to cover the tortillas, until the tortillas are gently browned and the cheese starts to melt, 2 to 3 minutes. With a very large spatula or two smaller ones, gently turn the quesadilla. Cook for 2 to 3 minutes more. Gently place the cooked quesadilla on a flat surface, such as a large cutting board, and cut into quarters with a sharp knife. Remove the grill pan from the heat to cool slightly.

5. Repeat with the second set of tortillas, using the remaining canola oil to oil the grill pan. Serve immediately.

Storage: *Refrigerate leftovers, tightly wrapped in aluminum foil, for up to 1 day.*

PER SERVING: 495 calories; 21g protein; 25g total fat; 2g fiber; 42g carbohydrates; 59mg cholesterol; 700mg sodium

Bean Quesadillas

MAKES: 8 QUESADILLA WEDGES (¼ QUESADILLA EACH)
PREPARATION TIME: 15 MINUTES

Quesadillas are typically cheese-filled tortillas, but this easy version
uses store-bought bean dip, salsa, and green onions. This version is
vegetarian, but you can add shredded chicken, beef, or pork if you
prefer. I like Rudi's gluten-free tortillas for this dish because the texture
is pliable and they are available in several flavors.

   4 Rudi's gluten-free flour tortillas
   ½ cup store-bought gluten-free bean dip or homemade Pinto Bean Dip
      (page 77)
   4 green onions, very thinly sliced
   2 tablespoons chopped fresh cilantro
   ½ teaspoon ground cumin (optional)
   ½ cup store-bought gluten-free Mexican salsa

1. Lay 2 of the tortillas on a flat surface and spread each evenly
with 2 tablespoons of the bean dip, and then sprinkle with the green
onions and cilantro. Top with the remaining 2 tortillas, pressing down
firmly to meld them together.

2. Lightly coat a nonstick skillet (gray, not black) with cooking
spray. Place a quesadilla in the skillet and toast over medium heat
until golden brown on the bottom. Flip carefully with a spatula and
toast on the other side. Lightly dust with cumin, if using. Remove
to a cutting board, cover with aluminum foil to keep warm, and set
aside until the second quesadilla is toasted. With a pizza cutter, cut
the quesadilla into 8 pieces and transfer to a serving plate. Repeat
with second quesadilla. Serve immediately, with Mexican salsa for
dipping.

Storage: *Refrigerate leftovers, wrapped in aluminum foil, for up to
1 day.*

PER ¼ QUESADILLA: 145 calories; 4g protein; 4g total fat; 2g fiber;
24g carbohydrates; 0mg cholesterol; 328mg sodium

Shrimp Tostadas with Chipotle Sauce

MAKES: 8 TOSTADAS   **PREPARATION TIME:** 10 MINUTES
WARMING TIME: 5 TO 10 MINUTES

Bright, colorful, and enticing—store-bought ingredients make this dish superfast, so keep them on hand for a quick appetizer or light meal. Vegetarians can omit the shrimp. You control the level of heat with the tomato salsa you choose, but it is also wonderful with salsa verde—a green salsa made from tomatillos.

- 8 gluten-free tostada shells
- 1 container (9 ounces) gluten-free bean dip

CHIPOTLE SAUCE

- ½ cup low-fat sour cream or sour cream alternative
- 1 tablespoon lime juice, or more to taste
- ½ teaspoon honey or agave nectar
- ¼ teaspoon chipotle chile powder, or to taste
- ½ cup chopped red onion
- 2 plum tomatoes or 8 cherry tomatoes, cored and diced
- 8 ounces cooked shrimp, tails removed and chopped
- 1 medium avocado, pitted, peeled, and diced
- 2 cups chopped iceberg lettuce
- ½ cup chopped fresh cilantro
- ½ cup store-bought gluten-free Mexican salsa or salsa verde

1. Place racks in the middle and lower third of the oven. Preheat the oven to 300°F. Place the tostada shells on two 9×13-inch rimmed baking sheets (the shells may overlap a little). Spread each shell with a scant 2 tablespoons of bean dip. Place one sheet on each rack in the oven to warm, 5 to 10 minutes, while preparing the remaining ingredients.

2. MAKE THE CHIPOTLE SAUCE: In a small bowl, whisk together the sour cream, lime juice, honey, and chipotle chile powder to make a smooth sauce, adding enough lime juice to reach a thin consistency.

3. Remove the tostadas from the oven. Top each tostada with equal amounts of onion, tomatoes, shrimp, avocado, lettuce, and cilantro. Drizzle with the chipotle sauce and serve immediately with the Mexican salsa.

Storage: *These tostadas are best eaten immediately.*

PER TOSTADA: 250 calories; 12g fat; 11g protein; 4g fiber; 27g carbohydrates; 58 mg cholesterol; 345mg sodium

English Muffin Pepperoni Pizzas

MAKES: 4 SERVINGS   **PREPARATION TIME:** 5 MINUTES
BAKING TIME: 5 TO 10 MINUTES

English muffins form the crust for these cute little pizzas. If you use store-bought marinara sauce and keep a stash of store-bought English muffins on hand, these snacks can be ready in just a few minutes.

  4 gluten-free English muffins, split in half
  ¾ cup store bought gluten-free marinara sauce
  2 cups shredded mozzarella cheese or cheese alternative
24 slices gluten-free pepperoni

1. Place a rack in the middle of the oven. Preheat the oven to 375°F.

2. Place the English muffin halves, cut side up, on a 9×13-inch nonstick baking sheet (gray, not black). Spoon 3 tablespoons of the marinara sauce on each half. Top each with ¼ cup of the mozzarella and 3 slices of pepperoni.

3. Bake for 5 to 10 minutes, until the cheese is melted. Serve hot.

Storage: *Refrigerate leftovers, tightly wrapped in aluminum foil, for up to 3 days.*

PER SERVING: 395 calories; 21g fat; 10g protein; 2g fiber; 32g carbohydrates; 910mg cholesterol; 59mg sodium

Thai Chicken Salad Wraps

MAKES: 4 WRAPS **PREPARATION TIME:** 10 MINUTES

This is a simple chicken salad wrap dressed up with Thai flavors—crunchiness from the almonds, spicy heat from the Thai curry paste, and sweetness from the pineapple.

¼ cup mayonnaise

2 tablespoons grated fresh ginger

2 tablespoons honey

2 tablespoons lime juice

2 tablespoons low-fat sour cream or sour cream alternative

1 teaspoon Thai red curry paste

1½ cups finely diced or shredded cooked chicken

½ cup pineapple tidbits, drained

¼ cup chopped fresh cilantro

¼ cup slivered almonds

4 Rudi's gluten-free flour tortillas

1 cup baby spinach

1. In a medium bowl, stir together the mayonnaise, ginger, honey, lime juice, sour cream, curry paste, chicken, pineapple, cilantro, and almonds until blended.

2. Soften the tortillas (see below) and immediately lay the tortillas on parchment paper on a flat surface.

3. Spread one-quarter of the chicken salad over each tortilla. Top with ¼ cup spinach. Gently roll each tortilla into a loose roll, then cut in half diagonally. Serve immediately.

Storage: Refrigerate leftovers, tightly wrapped in aluminum foil, for up to 1 day.

PER WRAP: 550 calories; 25g fat; 26g protein; 4g fiber; 58g carbohydrates; 50mg cholesterol; 514mg sodium

HOW TO SOFTEN TORTILLAS

Gluten-free flour tortillas can become rigid when stale or refrigerated, so they have a tendency to tear. To make them pliable, steam each tortilla on a splatter guard set over a skillet of barely simmering water, covered with a lid, until soft and pliable, 5 to 10 seconds. Place the steamed tortillas between sheets of parchment paper to keep them warm and soft while steaming the remaining tortillas.

Sloppy Joes

MAKES: 4 SERVINGS   PREPARATION TIME: 10 MINUTES
COOKING TIME: 20 TO 25 MINUTES

Keep gluten-free hamburger buns on hand and a stash of browned ground beef in your freezer, and these flavorful Sloppy Joes can be on the table pronto! Just remember to thaw the beef in the fridge the night before or have browned beef in the freezer and you will save even more time on this already quick meal. Serve with fresh veggies—such as celery sticks—and everyone will be happy.

    1 pound lean ground beef
  ½ cup finely diced onion
    1 cup ketchup
    2 tablespoons red wine vinegar
    1 tablespoon yellow mustard
    1 tablespoon gluten-free Worcestershire sauce
    1 garlic clove, minced
    1 teaspoon chopped fresh oregano or ½ teaspoon dried
  ½ teaspoon chili powder
  ½ teaspoon celery salt
       Pinch of ground cloves
    4 gluten-free hamburger buns

1. In a large, heavy skillet, cook the ground beef until deeply browned and dry, 5 to 7 minutes. (If starting with already cooked and browned ground beef, place it in the skillet.)

2. Add the onion, ketchup, vinegar, mustard, Worcestershire sauce, garlic, oregano, chili powder, celery salt, and cloves and bring to a boil. Reduce the heat to low, stir, and simmer, covered, for 15 minutes or until the meat is hot and the sauce has blended with the meat. Serve immediately on buns.

Storage: *Refrigerate leftover filling in a glass bowl, tightly covered, for up to 3 days. Or, freeze for up to 1 month in a freezer container.*

PER SANDWICH: 500 calories; 26g fat; 25g protein; 3g fiber; 41g carbohydrates; 85mg cholesterol; 614mg sodium

Creamy White Bean Dip

MAKES: 4 SERVINGS (ABOUT ¼ CUP EACH)   PREPARATION TIME: 5 MINUTES

Keeping canned beans on hand means you're always ready to make this simple dip—similar to hummus—which is much healthier than the typical fat-laden mayonnaise or sour cream–based dips. This naturally gluten-free dip is a delicious way to add variety and get important nutrients and fiber into a gluten-free diet. Serve with gluten-free crackers.

- 1 (14.5-ounce) can cannellini beans or navy beans, rinsed and drained
- 2 tablespoons lemon juice
- 2 tablespoons extra-virgin olive oil, or 1 tablespoon olive oil and 1 tablespoon sesame oil
- ½ teaspoon ground cumin
- ¼ teaspoon garlic powder
- ¼ teaspoon salt
- ¼ teaspoon freshly ground black pepper
- 2 teaspoons chopped fresh parsley or ½ teaspoon dried

1. In a food processor, combine the beans, lemon juice, oil, cumin, garlic powder, salt, and pepper. Process until the beans are mashed. Scrape down the side of the bowl and process again until the mixture is smooth.

2. Transfer the dip to a decorative serving bowl and garnish with the parsley. If not serving immediately, chill, covered, until serving time. Bring to room temperature before serving.

Storage: Refrigerate leftover dip in the serving bowl, tightly wrapped, for up to 3 days. Bring to room temperature before serving.

PER SERVING: 185 calories; 8g protein; 7g total fat; 5g fiber; 24g carbohydrates; 0mg cholesterol; 139mg sodium

Pinto Bean Dip

MAKES: 4 SERVINGS (GENEROUS ¼ CUP EACH)   PREPARATION TIME: 5 MINUTES

You can certainly buy pinto bean dips, but this homemade version has an unsurpassed fresh flavor. This naturally gluten-free dip is a delicious way to get important nutrients and fiber into a gluten-free diet. Serve it with store-bought gluten-free tortilla chips or use it in recipes that call for bean dip (such as the Bean Quesadillas on page 69).

- 1 (15-ounce) can pinto beans, rinsed and drained
- 1 tablespoon hot water, plus more if necessary
- 1 teaspoon extra-virgin olive oil
- 1 garlic clove, chopped
- ¼ teaspoon salt
- 1 teaspoon fresh oregano or ½ teaspoon dried
- 1 teaspoon chili powder
- ½ teaspoon ground cumin
- ½ teaspoon ground coriander
- ¼ cup chopped fresh cilantro, plus more for garnish
- ¼ cup chopped green onions, plus more for garnish

In a food processor, combine the beans, water, oil, garlic, salt, oregano, chili powder, cumin, and coriander. Blend until smooth, adding another tablespoon or so of hot water if the mixture is too stiff for spreading or dipping. Transfer to a shallow serving bowl, garnish with the cilantro and green onions, and serve.

Storage: *Refrigerate leftover dip in the serving bowl, tightly wrapped, for up to 3 days. Bring to room temperature before serving.*

PER SERVING: 95 calories; 5g protein; 2g total fat; 4g fiber; 16g carbohydrates; 0mg cholesterol; 569mg sodium

Crab Cocktail Spread

MAKES: 4 SERVINGS (ABOUT ½ CUP EACH)   PREPARATION TIME: 5 MINUTES

This retro favorite is delicious and so easy to put together at the last minute—if you keep the ingredients on hand, plus a package of gluten-free crackers to serve with the spread.

- 1 (8-ounce) package cream cheese or cream cheese alternative, at room temperature
- ½ cup store-bought gluten-free cocktail sauce
- 1 (7.5-ounce) can lump crabmeat, picked over

Place the softened cream cheese on a serving plate and drizzle the cocktail sauce on top. Gently place the crab meat on top, and serve.

Storage: *Refrigerate leftovers, tightly covered, for up to 1 day.*

PER SERVING: 205 calories; 16g protein; 11g total fat; 0g fiber; 10g carbohydrates; 73mg cholesterol; 794mg sodium

UPDATED CRAB COCKTAIL

This retro appetizer was first popular decades ago, but it has never left my repertoire because it is still delicious. If you would like to update it, swap the cocktail sauce for Major Grey's mango chutney or red pepper jelly. The sharp, spicy sweetness of the chutney or jelly contrasts nicely with the velvety cream cheese and provides a boldly flavored accent to the rich, savory crab.

Stuffed Dates

MAKES: 8 SERVINGS   PREPARATION TIME: 5 MINUTES

The hardest part of this simple appetizer is slitting the dates and removing the pits. Once that's done, it's a breeze to stuff them. Dates and almonds are so flavorful and add fiber and nutrients to your diet, and the little strip of Swiss cheese (or cheese alternative) adds just the right savory contrast. These appetizers can be made ahead and chilled. Bring to room temperature before serving.

- 16 whole dates
- 1 slice Swiss cheese, cut into ⅛-inch strips (or equivalent amounts of cheese alternative)
- 16 small whole almonds

With a paring knife, slit each date lengthwise from end to end and remove the pit. Place a strip of cheese and an almond inside each date and press shut. Arrange on a serving plate or in a small bowl, and serve.

Storage: *Refrigerate leftovers, tightly wrapped, for up to 1 week.*

PER SERVING: 130 calories; 5g protein; 7g total fat; 2g fiber; 14g carbohydrates; 13mg cholesterol; 38mg sodium

Loaded Potato Skins

MAKES: 8 SERVINGS   **PREPARATION TIME:** 15 MINUTES
BROILING TIME: 8 TO 12 MINUTES

This recipe is a fantastic crowd-pleaser. You do have to plan ahead by roasting the potatoes in advance (perhaps when making another night's dinner?) and keeping cooked bacon strips in the freezer. I prefer smaller russets, about 3 inches long, which gives you more crispy skin in proportion to the soft interior. If you can't find them, cut large, baked russets into quarters and scoop a hole in the flesh to hold the fillings. For a vegetarian version, omit the bacon and top with chopped tomatoes, slices of avocado, or black olives—added after the final broiling.

- 8 small (3-inch) cooked russet potatoes (about 2¼ pounds), at room temperature
- 2 tablespoons olive oil
  Salt and freshly ground black pepper to taste
- 1 cup shredded cheddar cheese or cheese alternative (8 ounces)
- 4 bacon slices, cooked and crumbled
- ½ cup sour cream or sour cream alternative
- 2 green onions, including green tops, thinly sliced

1. Place a rack in the middle of the oven. Preheat the oven to broil. Slice each cooked potato in half lengthwise (or cut into quarters if using large russets). Scoop out the flesh with a spoon, leaving about ¼ inch of flesh along the skin. (Use the flesh for another use.) Brush both sides of the potatoes with the olive oil and season with salt and pepper. Place the potato skins, cut side down, on a rimmed baking sheet.

2. Broil until the skins start to crisp, 3 to 5 minutes (watch closely so they don't burn). Flip the skins over and broil until the top edges just start to brown, 2 to 3 minutes more. Remove from the oven and sprinkle the cheese evenly in the potato skins.

3. Return the potato skins to the oven and broil just until the cheese starts to melt, 2 to 3 minutes. Remove the potato skins from the oven and sprinkle with the bacon. Dot each with 1½ teaspoons of sour cream and a sprinkle of green onions. Serve immediately.

Storage: *Refrigerate leftovers in a glass container, tightly covered, for up to 3 days.*

PER SERVING: 330 calories; 14g protein; 20g total fat; 2g fiber; 23g carbohydrates; 43mg cholesterol; 414mg sodium

Brie with Honey and Chopped Nuts

MAKES: 4 SERVINGS   PREPARATION TIME: 2 MINUTES

The creamy smoothness of Brie pairs nicely with sweet honey, while crunchy nuts provide a bit of contrasting texture. Dairy-sensitive? Use Daiya's cheddar-style wedges instead, but it is softer than Brie, so just bring it to room temperature rather than heating in the microwave. Serve with gluten-free crackers.

- 1 small round Brie cheese (about 6.5 ounces) or 8 ounces Daiya cheddar-style wedges
- 2 tablespoons honey
- 2 tablespoons chopped walnuts, pecans, or almonds
- 2 crisp apples (such as Gala or Braeburn), cored and cut into ¼-inch slices

1. Place the Brie on a microwave-safe serving plate and heat gently in the microwave on Low power for 1 to 2 minutes, just until it is slightly softened and can be easily cut or spread with a knife. Don't make it too hot or it will melt all over the plate.

2. Pour the honey over the Brie and sprinkle the chopped nuts on top. Serve with the sliced apples alongside.

Storage: Once the cheese is warmed and drizzled with honey, it's best to eat immediately.

PER SERVING: 250 calories; 11g protein; 15g total fat; 2g fiber; 20g carbohydrates; 46mg cholesterol; 290mg sodium

Grains, Beans, and Pasta

GRAINS
Coconut Rice
Slow Cooker Brown Rice Risotto
Easy Soft Polenta
Hazelnut-Quinoa Salad

BEANS
Quick Baked Beans
Spicy Black Beans
Cannellini Beans with Wilted Spinach
Warm Lentils with Herbs
Split Pea Dal with Rice
Slow Cooker Red Beans with Rice

PASTA
Linguine with Toasted Almonds
Pesto Penne
Lighter Fettuccine Alfredo
Penne alla Vodka
Spaghetti Carbonara
Linguine with Red Clam Sauce

Coconut Rice

MAKES: 4 SERVINGS   **PREPARATION TIME:** 20 MINUTES

Use this flavorful recipe to cure the "white rice is boring" syndrome at dinnertime. This side dish is especially nice when served with an Asian, Indian, or Southwestern-inspired main dish. I prefer the larger raw coconut flakes, available at health food stores, but you can also use unsweetened shredded coconut. Make this vegetarian by replacing the chicken broth with vegetable broth.

- 1 tablespoon canola oil
- 1 cup white basmati rice
- 2 cups gluten-free low-sodium vegetable broth (or chicken broth)
- ½ teaspoon salt, or to taste
- ¼ teaspoon gluten-free Asian spice blend
- 1 cup unsweetened coconut flakes
- 2 tablespoons chopped fresh parsley or 1 tablespoon dried

1. In a large, heavy saucepan, heat the oil over medium heat. Add the rice, broth, salt, and spice blend and cook, covered, for 15 to 20 minutes, until the rice is tender.

2. Remove the pan from the heat. Stir in the coconut flakes and serve hot, garnished with the parsley.

Storage: Refrigerate leftovers in a glass container, tightly sealed, for up to 2 days.

PER SERVING: 340 calories; 11g protein; 17g total fat; 3g fiber; 38g carbohydrates; 0mg cholesterol; 564mg sodium

Slow Cooker Brown Rice Risotto

MAKES: 4 SERVINGS (½ CUP EACH)   PREPARATION TIME: 5 MINUTES
SLOW COOKER TIME: 6 TO 8 HOURS

Risotto has the unfortunate reputation of being a labor-intensive, time-consuming dish. But my easy slow cooker method using nutritious brown rice rather than Arborio rice makes it possible for even the busiest cook. A half cup of cooked brown rice equals a serving of whole grain, so this dish helps you reach your daily goal of three to five servings. It produces a fairly robust, stiff risotto with lots of chew and texture; stir in more broth after cooking for a looser texture. Serve risotto as a side dish, or use chicken broth and add cooked shrimp or chicken cubes to make it an entrée.

1 teaspoon extra-virgin olive oil
½ cup chopped onion or 2 teaspoons dried minced onion
½ cup brown rice
1 (14.5-ounce) can or 1¾ cups gluten-free low-sodium vegetable
  broth (or chicken broth)
⅛ teaspoon salt
¼ cup grated Parmesan cheese or soy Parmesan

1. Lightly coat the inside crock of a 4-quart slow cooker with cooking spray. Add the olive oil, onion, rice, broth, and salt to the slow cooker and stir to blend thoroughly.

2. Cover and cook on Low for 6 to 8 hours, until the broth is absorbed and the rice is tender. Stir in the Parmesan cheese and serve hot.

Storage: Refrigerate leftovers, tightly covered, for up to 1 day.

PER SERVING: 145 calories; 9g protein; 3g total fat; 1g fiber; 21g carbohydrates; 4mg cholesterol; 374mg sodium

Easy Soft Polenta

MAKES: 4 SERVINGS (¾ CUP EACH AS A SIDE DISH)   PREPARATION TIME: 2 MINUTES
COOKING TIME: 20 MINUTES

Polenta is Italian cornmeal, but Bob's Red Mill brand also calls it corn grits on the label. Most polentas require your total attention, standing over the stovetop while stirring the polenta to keep it from getting lumpy and trying to prevent it from splattering. My easy no-stir method eliminates the mess by cooking the polenta in a very large bowl in the microwave—saving you time by freeing you to prepare the rest of the meal. Polenta is perfect served under Pork Cutlets with Marsala Wine and Mushrooms (page 124), but it can also be a side dish for vegetarian meals if you use vegetable broth.

    1 cup Bob's Red Mill gluten-free polenta/corn grits
3½ cups gluten-free low-sodium vegetable broth (or chicken broth)
    1 tablespoon butter or buttery spread
    ¼ cup grated Parmesan cheese or soy Parmesan
    ½ teaspoon salt, or to taste

1. In a large, microwave-safe bowl, whisk all of the ingredients together. I use an 8-cup glass Pyrex measuring cup—large enough to avoid boil-overs.

2. Lay a sheet of waxed paper over the bowl and cook in the microwave on High power in 10-minute increments, whisking between each increment, to reach the desired consistency. Cooking times may vary depending on your microwave; mine takes two 10-minute periods for this recipe, for a total of 20 minutes. Serve immediately, because it starts to firm up as it cools.

Storage: Refrigerate leftovers, tightly sealed, for up to 3 days.

PER SERVING: 235 calories; 15g protein; 5g total fat; 5g fiber; 33g carbohydrates; 12mg cholesterol; 814mg sodium

Hazelnut-Quinoa Salad

MAKES: 4 SERVINGS AS A MAIN COURSE OR 8 SERVINGS AS AN APPETIZER
PREPARATION TIME: 15 MINUTES

My friend and colleague Lori Sobelson, director of program outreach at Bob's Red Mill, is passionate about nutritious food—such as her delicious quinoa salad, which can be served as a main dish or side dish. Quinoa is a nutty-tasting, super-nutritious whole grain that contains all of the essential amino acids and can be served in place of rice. To save time, prepare the dressing and cook the quinoa the night before and refrigerate. Meat eaters can add chopped cooked chicken or cooked shrimp for more protein.

DRESSING

- 1/3 cup orange juice
- 1/4 cup strawberry fruit spread
- 3 tablespoons balsamic vinegar or white balsamic vinegar
- 2 tablespoons canola oil
- 1 tablespoon soft silken tofu
- 1 medium garlic clove, minced
- 3/4 teaspoon salt

SALAD

- 2 cups cooked red or white quinoa
- 1/4 cup hazelnuts, toasted and coarsely crushed (see page 98)
- 1/4 cup green onions, finely chopped
- 1/2 cup halved red seedless grapes

1. MAKE THE DRESSING: In a food processor or blender, combine all of the ingredients. Blend for about 1 minute or until smooth. Set aside.

2. MAKE THE SALAD: In a medium bowl, combine all of the ingredients. Pour 1/2 to 3/4 cup of the dressing over the quinoa mixture and toss to coat it thoroughly. Refrigerate any remaining dressing and use within 2 weeks. Serve the salad immediately at room temperature or chill for 2 hours to serve cold.

Storage: Refrigerate leftovers, tightly sealed, for up to 2 days.

PER MAIN-COURSE SERVING: 350 calories; 7g protein; 15g total fat; 4g fiber; 50g carbohydrates; 0mg cholesterol; 420mg sodium

USING SUBSTITUTES IN WHOLE-GRAIN SALADS

It is easy to make substitutes for the various ingredients in this wholesome salad. Though quinoa is not a whole grain but technically a seed (related to buckwheat and Swiss chard), it can be replaced with 2 cups of cooked whole grains such as brown rice, sorghum, or millet. Instead of hazelnuts, use walnuts, almonds, pecans, or pumpkin seeds. The grapes can be replaced with sliced oranges, chopped fresh figs, or diced fresh apples. Or instead of fresh fruits, use dried fruits, such as blueberries, cherries, cranberries, figs, or prunes. The creative possibilities are endless with recipes such as this one, so use what you have in your pantry.

Quick Baked Beans

MAKES: 4 SERVINGS   PREPARATION TIME: 5 MINUTES

This tastes very much like your honest-to-goodness, authentic, cooked-from-scratch baked beans—the kind you soak all night and then cook all the next day so you can eat them that night. Instead, my "speed-scratch" microwave version takes 5 minutes with your favorite store-bought ingredients. Use the best-quality products you can find, since there are only three ingredients. Enjoy!

    2 (14.5-ounce) cans pork and beans, rinsed and thoroughly drained
    ¾ cup gluten-free barbecue sauce
    1 teaspoon dried minced onion

In a large bowl, toss the beans with the barbecue sauce and onion until thoroughly blended. Place the mixture in a medium saucepan and heat over medium heat, or place in a microwave-safe serving bowl and heat to serving temperature. Serve immediately.

Storage: Refrigerate leftovers, tightly sealed, for up to 3 days.

PER SERVING: 255 calories; 12g protein; 4g total fat; 12g fiber; 47g carbohydrates; 14mg cholesterol; 384mg sodium

Spicy Black Beans

MAKES: 4 SERVINGS   PREPARATION TIME: 5 MINUTES   COOKING TIME: 15 MINUTES

I always have cans of black beans in the pantry, ready to turn into a side dish, soup, or bean dip. This easy version can be whipped up in less than 10 minutes. If you want the beans a little less spicy, cut the chili powder in half. Serve with Southwestern dishes such as tacos, fajitas, or Southwestern-style wraps—as a filling or as a side dish.

- 1 (14.5-ounce) can black beans, rinsed and drained
- 1 cup gluten-free low-sodium chicken broth
- 1 tablespoon extra-virgin olive oil
- 1 smoked pork chop, bone removed and extra fat trimmed, cut into ½-inch cubes
- 1 teaspoon dried minced onion
- 2 garlic cloves, minced, or ¼ teaspoon garlic powder
- 1 bay leaf
- ¼ teaspoon chili powder
- ¼ teaspoon salt
- ¼ teaspoon freshly ground black pepper
- 1 tablespoon chopped fresh cilantro

In a medium saucepan, combine the beans, broth, oil, pork, onion, garlic, bay leaf, chili powder, salt, and pepper. Bring to a boil over medium-high heat, then reduce the heat to low and cook, covered, for 15 minutes. Remove the bay leaf and serve hot, sprinkled with the cilantro.

Storage: *Refrigerate leftovers, tightly covered, for up to 3 days.*

PER SERVING: 190 calories; 14g protein; 8g total fat; 6g fiber; 15g carbohydrates; 18mg cholesterol; 594mg sodium

Cannellini Beans with Wilted Spinach

MAKES: 4 SERVINGS   PREPARATION TIME: 10 MINUTES

Savvy cooks keep a variety of canned beans in the pantry so they're always ready to make quick, healthy dishes. I prefer cannellini beans (white kidney beans) for this recipe because they hold their shape nicely and look pretty with the dark green spinach. Beans are a marvelous source of fiber and protein and—along with the nutrients in spinach—they make an extremely healthy and naturally gluten-free choice. A fillet of grilled salmon would be the perfect way to add protein to this already healthy dish, and then drizzle it with a little extra olive oil. Or serve it alongside Steak Diane (page 112).

  2 tablespoons extra-virgin olive oil
  2 tablespoons butter or buttery spread
  1 (15-ounce) can cannellini beans, rinsed and drained
  2 garlic cloves, minced
  ¼ teaspoon crushed red pepper, or to taste
  2 (9-ounce) packages ready-to-eat baby spinach
  ¼ cup grated Parmesan cheese or soy Parmesan
  ⅛ teaspoon salt
  ⅛ teaspoon freshly ground black pepper

1. In a large deep skillet, heat the oil and butter over medium heat. Add the beans, garlic, and crushed red pepper and simmer for 5 minutes.

2. Reduce the heat to medium-low, add the spinach, cover, and simmer just until the spinach is wilted, 3 to 4 minutes. Stir in the Parmesan cheese. Add salt and pepper and serve hot.

Storage: Refrigerate leftovers, tightly covered, for up to 1 day.

PER SERVING: 330 calories; 18g protein; 15g total fat; 11g fiber; 36g carbohydrates; 19mg cholesterol; 270mg sodium

Warm Lentils with Herbs

MAKES: 4 SERVINGS   PREPARATION TIME: 5 MINUTES
COOKING TIME: 25 TO 30 MINUTES

Lentils cook more quickly than beans, so they are a good choice for busy cooks. They are often served in sophisticated restaurants as a base under elegant roasts, rack of lamb, or pork chops because they soak up those wonderful juices from the meat. Or, serve them alongside the main dish. To save precious minutes at mealtime, chop and store the onion, tomatoes, and fresh herbs the night before. Make this dish vegetarian by using vegetable broth.

- 1 cup brown, red, or yellow lentils
- 1 cup gluten-free low-sodium vegetable broth (or chicken broth)
- ¼ cup diced yellow onion
- ½ teaspoon salt
- 1 garlic clove, minced
- 2 ripe plum tomatoes, diced
- 2 tablespoons chopped fresh basil or thyme or 1½ teaspoons dried
- 2 tablespoons chopped fresh parsley or 1½ teaspoons dried
- 2 tablespoons extra-virgin olive oil
- 1 tablespoon sherry or champagne vinegar
  Salt and freshly ground black pepper to taste

1. In a medium saucepan, combine the lentils, broth, onion, salt, and garlic. Bring to a boil over medium heat, then reduce the heat to low and simmer, covered, for 25 to 30 minutes, until the lentils are soft.

2. Stir in the tomatoes, basil, parsley, oil, and vinegar and heat to serving temperature. Add salt and pepper to taste. Serve hot.

Storage: Refrigerate leftovers, tightly covered, for up to 4 days.

PER SERVING: 245 calories; 17g protein; 7g total fat; 15g fiber; 31g carbohydrates; 0mg cholesterol; 405mg sodium

Split Pea Dal with Rice

MAKES: 4 SERVINGS   PREPARATION TIME: 5 MINUTES
COOKING TIME: 25 TO 30 MINUTES

In India, dal or dahl refers to any type of lentil, bean, or legume, and it sometimes refers to soup or stew made with legumes. My version is a lightly spiced stew served over hot cooked rice. Legumes are particularly high in protein and fiber, and they can be seasoned and served in so many ways. Although there are a number of spices here, they blend beautifully to make the lovely Indian flavors we all love. This is such a simple, tasty, nutritious dish that once you buy the spices, you will want to make it often. Save time by measuring the spices the night before. Meat lovers may add chopped chicken along with the split peas for a fuller meal.

1 tablespoon canola oil
1 teaspoon ground coriander
1 teaspoon ground cumin
1 teaspoon ground turmeric
¼ teaspoon ground ginger
¼ teaspoon salt
⅛ teaspoon cayenne pepper
1 garlic clove, minced
1½ cups green or red split peas
4 cups water
2 tablespoons lemon juice
4 cups hot, cooked brown or white rice

1. In a stockpot, heat the oil over medium heat and add the coriander, cumin, turmeric, and ginger, stirring constantly for 1 minute. Add the salt, cayenne, garlic, split peas, and water.

2. Bring to a boil, then reduce the heat to medium-low and simmer, covered, for 25 to 30 minutes, until the peas are tender and the mixture thickens slightly. Stir in the lemon juice. Serve immediately over hot cooked rice.

Storage: *Refrigerate leftovers, tightly covered, for up to 4 days.*

PER SERVING: 510 calories; 33g protein; 6g total fat; 22g fiber; 92g carbohydrates; 0mg cholesterol; 155mg sodium

Slow Cooker Red Beans with Rice

MAKES: 4 SERVINGS   PREPARATION TIME: 10 MINUTES
SLOW COOKER TIME: 6 TO 8 HOURS

You can cook this dish in a pot on the stovetop, but it is so much easier to let a slow cooker do the job for you. To really speed things up, plan ahead to have cooked brown rice waiting in the fridge for a quick reheat. I use a salt-free Cajun seasoning by Spice Islands; if your seasoning contains salt, reduce the recipe's salt to ½ teaspoon, or to taste. Leftovers are great!

- 1 small yellow onion, chopped
- 1 celery stalk, chopped
- 2 garlic cloves, minced
- 2½ to 3 teaspoons gluten-free Cajun seasoning blend
- 1 teaspoon salt
- 2 tablespoons brown sugar
- 2 dashes hot pepper sauce, or to taste
- 2 gluten-free andouille sausage links, cut into ½-inch rounds
- 1 cup dried red beans (not kidney beans)
- 4 cups water
- 4 cups hot, cooked brown rice
- 1 tablespoon chopped fresh parsley or cilantro

1. Place the onion, celery, garlic, Cajun seasoning, salt, brown sugar, hot pepper sauce, and sausage in a 4-quart slow cooker.

2. Pick over the beans to remove stones or debris, then rinse thoroughly and add to the slow cooker. Add the water and simmer on Low for 6 to 8 hours, until the water is absorbed and the beans and rice are tender. Taste and add more hot pepper sauce, if desired. Serve over hot cooked brown rice, sprinkled with the parsley.

Storage: *Refrigerate leftovers, tightly covered, for up to 4 days.*

PER SERVING: 495 calories; 10g protein; 8g total fat; 17g fiber; 89g carbohydrates; 10mg cholesterol; 798mg sodium

PASTA

Linguine with Toasted Almonds

MAKES: 4 SERVINGS   **PREPARATION TIME:** UNDER 15 MINUTES

If you toast the nuts beforehand, this dish comes together as soon as the pasta is done. I can boil water in 90 seconds with my induction stovetop, so I cook pasta very quickly. But even with traditional gas or electric stovetops, this is a quick entrée; have all the side dishes ready when you start preparing the meal. The nuts provide protein, but cooked shrimp is also a nice addition.

- 4 cups water
- Salt, as needed
- 8 ounces gluten-free linguine
- ¼ cup toasted slivered almonds, pine nuts, or chopped walnuts (see below)
- 1 tablespoon chopped fresh parsley
- 1 teaspoon lemon pepper
- 2 tablespoons olive oil
- ¼ cup grated Parmesan cheese or soy Parmesan

1. In a large pot, bring the water to a boil and add salt liberally. Add the pasta and cook according to the package directions until al dente, 8 to 12 minutes, depending on the brand. Avoid overcooking because pasta continues to cook after it is removed from the heat.

2. Drain the linguine and toss with the almonds, parsley, lemon pepper, olive oil, and Parmesan cheese. Serve immediately.

Storage: *Refrigerate leftovers, tightly covered, for up to 2 days.*

PER SERVING: 350 calories; 11g protein; 14g total fat; 2g fiber; 45g carbohydrates; 4mg cholesterol; 457mg sodium

HOW TO TOAST NUTS

Place a rack in the middle of the oven. Preheat the oven to 325°F. Place the nuts in a thin layer on a 9×13-inch baking sheet (not nonstick). Bake for 5 minutes, then watch for browning as you bake for another 5 to 8 minutes. Some nuts will brown more quickly than others, so if you use a blend of different types of nuts, you may have to toast them separately. Let cool, and then chop.

Pesto Penne

MAKES: 4 SERVINGS   PREPARATION TIME: UNDER 15 MINUTES

Penne is my favorite pasta because it holds its shape and is easier to
eat than spaghetti—especially for kids. Store-bought pesto saves time,
but homemade pesto is easy to make in a food processor. This is a
wonderful dish for vegetarians, but you can boost the protein content
by adding ½-inch cubes of cooked chicken or cooked shrimp—in
whatever amounts you like.

    8 cups water
      Salt, as needed
    1 pound gluten-free penne
    ½ cup Homemade Basil Pesto (see page 100) or gluten-free basil pesto
    ¼ cup grated Parmesan cheese or soy Parmesan

1. In a large pot, bring the water to a boil and add salt liberally. Add
the pasta and cook according to the package directions until al dente,
8 to 12 minutes, depending on the brand. Avoid overcooking because
pasta continues to cook after it is removed from the heat.

2. Toss the cooked pasta with the pesto. Serve immediately, topped
with the Parmesan cheese.

Storage: *Refrigerate leftovers, tightly covered, for up to 1 day.*

PER SERVING: 580 calories; 21g protein; 16g total fat; 4g fiber; 85g carbohydrates;
13mg cholesterol; 314mg sodium

Homemade Basil Pesto

MAKES: ½ CUP

¼ cup pine nuts, toasted (see page 98)
2 cups lightly packed fresh basil
1 garlic clove, minced
⅓ cup extra-virgin olive oil
3 tablespoons grated Parmesan cheese or soy Parmesan
Salt and freshly ground black pepper to taste

1. In a food processor, process the pine nuts until they are finely ground. Add the basil and garlic and process just until a little bit of texture remains. With the food processor running, add the oil through the feed tube.

2. Remove the pesto from the food processor and stir in the Parmesan cheese and salt and pepper to taste.

Storage: Refrigerate in a glass jar with a tight lid for up to 1 day. Pour a thin layer of olive oil on top of the pesto to discourage browning.

HOW TO COOK GLUTEN-FREE PASTA

Use plenty of water—4 cups for each 8 ounces of pasta.

Salt the water liberally after it starts to boil—most pasta is mild, and salt brings out its flavor.

Put the pasta into boiling water and stir constantly until it comes to a boil again to prevent clumping.

Cook the pasta following the manufacturer's directions on the package because, unlike regular pasta—which is made from wheat—different brands of gluten-free pasta are made with different grains and therefore cook at different rates.

Cook the pasta just until it's al dente, or "to the tooth"; it will feel slightly soft when you bite into it but not overly so. Remove it from the heat and drain; it will continue to cook from residual heat even after it is out of the boiling water.

Unlike regular pasta, you need to serve cooked gluten-free pasta immediately; it will get mushy and clump together if it sits in the pot or on a buffet table for an extended period of time. It will separate when rinsed briefly with hot water.

Lighter Fettuccine Alfredo

MAKES: 4 SERVINGS   PREPARATION TIME: UNDER 15 MINUTES

Fettuccine Alfredo, typically made with heavy cream and butter, is a delicious dish, but it can be extremely high in fat and calories. My version uses less fattening ingredients without compromising the flavor. Of course, you can use any traditional fettuccine Alfredo recipe with gluten-free pasta. The texture of this dish will vary with the type of pasta you use—heavier and darker in color if you use rice bran pasta from Tinkyada; lighter in color if you use pasta from DeBoles.

    4 cups water
      Salt, as needed
    8 ounces gluten-free fettuccine
1½ cups low-fat cream cheese or cream cheese alternative
    3 tablespoons milk of choice
    ¼ cup grated Parmesan cheese or soy Parmesan
    1 small garlic clove, minced, or ⅛ teaspoon garlic powder
    2 tablespoons butter or buttery spread
    ¼ cup chopped fresh parsley (optional)
    1 teaspoon lemon pepper (optional)

1. In a large pot, bring the water to a boil, and add salt liberally. Add the pasta, and cook according to the package directions until al dente, 8 to 12 minutes, depending on the brand. Avoid overcooking because pasta continues to cook after it is removed from the heat.

2. While the pasta cooks, in a food processor, combine the cream cheese, milk, Parmesan cheese, garlic, and butter. Process until the sauce is very smooth.

3. Transfer the sauce to a heavy medium saucepan and whisk over medium heat until the sauce reaches serving temperature.

4. Drain the fettuccine, toss with the sauce, and serve topped with the chopped parsley and lemon pepper, if desired.

Storage: *Refrigerate leftovers, tightly covered, for up to 2 days.*

PER SERVING: 490 calories; 19g protein; 23g total fat; 2g fiber; 50g carbohydrates; 68mg cholesterol; 784mg sodium

Penne Alla Vodka

MAKES: 4 SERVINGS   PREPARATION TIME: UNDER 15 MINUTES

Although the title of this recipe may seem exotic, it is super-easy
to assemble. For delectable variations on this basic dish, see below.
Since vodka is distilled, gluten proteins cannot survive, so it is safe—
regardless of what the vodka is made from. You may use dry white
wine, but the resulting flavor will be somewhat different.

- 1 tablespoon butter, buttery spread, or canola oil
- 1 tablespoon olive oil
- 1 large shallot, minced
- 1 garlic clove, minced, or ⅛ teaspoon garlic powder
- 1 (14.5-ounce) can petite diced tomatoes, undrained
- ⅛ teaspoon sugar
- ¼ cup vodka or dry white wine
- ¼ cup heavy cream, whole milk, or plain soy milk
- 4 cups water
  Salt, as needed
- 8 ounces gluten-free penne

1. In a medium skillet, heat the butter and olive oil over medium
heat. Add the shallots and garlic and cook, stirring constantly, for
3 minutes, or until the shallots are soft. Add the tomatoes and sugar
and simmer for 5 minutes, or until the tomatoes reduce down and
thicken just slightly.

2. Stir in the vodka and cream and simmer the sauce gently over
very low heat until it reaches serving temperature, then remove it
from the heat. Cover and keep warm while the pasta cooks.

3. Meanwhile, bring the water to a boil in a large pot, and add
salt liberally. Add the pasta, and cook according to the package
directions until al dente, 8 to 12 minutes, depending on the brand.
Avoid overcooking because pasta continues to cook after it is
removed from the heat. Drain the pasta and serve immediately with
the sauce.

Storage: *Refrigerate leftovers, tightly sealed, for up to 3 days.*

PER SERVING: 365 calories; 8g protein; 12g total fat; 3g fiber; 48g carbohydrates;
28mg cholesterol; 16mg sodium

CONTINUED ON PAGE 104

CONTINUED FROM PAGE 103

PENNE ALLA VODKA WITH GREEN PEAS: Add 1 cup cooked green peas to the cream sauce and bring to serving temperature.

PENNE ALLA VODKA WITH SMOKED SALMON: Add 2 ounces smoked salmon, finely diced, to the cream sauce and bring to serving temperature.

MAKING PASTA DISHES HEARTIER

Just as this Penne Alla Vodka can be transformed into a more filling dish by adding smoked salmon, any of the meatless pasta dishes in this chapter can easily be made more substantial by adding your favorite beef, chicken, or seafood—in whatever proportions you like. Add precooked ingredients at the end of the cooking time to heat and blend together with the pasta and sauce. Or, if you're adding raw meat or chicken pieces that require cooking, add them to the sauce early enough to allow them time to cook through.

Spaghetti Carbonara

MAKES: 4 SERVINGS PREPARATION TIME: 20 MINUTES (DUE TO COOLING TIME)
COOKING TIME: 10 MINUTES

This classic Italian entrée is seldom available in a gluten-free version in restaurants, but don't let that stop you from enjoying it at home. It is basically pasta tossed with a rich cream sauce that is typically flavored with pancetta (uncured Italian bacon). But you can use regular cured bacon, which makes a more flavorful dish. Be sure to cool the skillet for 5 minutes or switch to a different (cool) skillet, or you'll get scrambled eggs instead of cream sauce.

- 4 cups water
- Salt, as needed
- 12 ounces gluten-free spaghetti or linguine
- 4 ounces pancetta or 4 bacon slices, diced
- 2 teaspoons sweet rice flour
- ¾ cup milk of choice
- 2 large egg yolks, beaten
- ½ cup grated Parmesan cheese or Pecorino Romano
- ½ teaspoon freshly ground black pepper

1. In a large pot, bring the water to a boil and add salt liberally. Add the pasta, and cook according to the package directions until al dente, 8 to 12 minutes, depending on the brand. Avoid overcooking because pasta continues to cook after it is removed from the heat. Reserve ½ cup of the hot pasta water in a small measuring cup, then drain the pasta. Leave the pasta in the colander.

2. While the pasta cooks, fry the pancetta in a large, heavy skillet over medium heat until crispy, 4 to 5 minutes. Drain on paper towels, leave the drippings in the skillet, and remove the skillet from the heat to let cool for 5 minutes—or transfer the drippings to a different, cool skillet.

3. In a small bowl, whisk the sweet rice flour into ¼ cup of the milk until smooth. Then whisk in the rest of the milk, the egg yolks, and ¼ teaspoon salt until the mixture is very smooth. Return the skillet to low heat, add the milk-egg mixture, and cook, whisking constantly to prevent the eggs from scrambling, until thickened, 2 to 3 minutes. Remove from the heat and stir in ¼ cup of the Parmesan cheese. Add enough of the reserved hot pasta water to make a smooth, pourable sauce.

4. To the skillet, add the drained pasta and pancetta and toss until the pasta is thoroughly coated. Serve immediately, topped with the remaining ¼ cup Parmesan cheese and the black pepper.

Storage: *Refrigerate leftovers, tightly covered, for up to 2 days.*

PER SERVING: 475 calories; 26g protein; 10g total fat; 2g fiber; 68g carbohydrates; 136mg cholesterol; 1,116mg sodium

Linguine with Red Clam Sauce

MAKES: 4 SERVINGS   PREPARATION TIME: UNDER 20 MINUTES

This meal comes together so quickly that you should have everything else ready before you start preparing it. All you really need to complete the meal is a crisp tossed salad and some gluten-free bread. Unlike most pasta recipes, the pasta cooks right in the sauce—rather than in water—which allows it to absorb more of the clam flavor.

1 tablespoon extra-virgin olive oil

½ cup diced onion

1 garlic clove, minced, or ⅛ teaspoon garlic powder

¼ teaspoon crushed red pepper

½ cup dry white wine

1 (14.5-ounce) can petite diced tomatoes, undrained

1 (6.5-ounce) can clams, undrained

½ teaspoon salt

8 ounces gluten-free linguine

2 tablespoons chopped fresh parsley

1 tablespoon grated Parmesan cheese or soy Parmesan

1. In a deep pot, heat the olive oil over medium heat. Add the onion and cook, stirring constantly, for 2 to 3 minutes, until the onion is soft. Add the garlic and crushed red pepper and cook for another minute.

2. Add the wine and cook until nearly evaporated, 2 to 3 minutes. Add the tomatoes, clams, and salt. Simmer, uncovered, for 5 minutes.

3. Add the linguine and gradually push it down into the sauce so it can cook in the sauce. Continue to simmer for 6 to 8 minutes or until the linguine is almost done. The starch from the linguine will thicken the sauce slightly as it cooks, and the linguine will continue to cook after removing it from the heat. Stir in the parsley and cook until the sauce thickens a bit more. (If the sauce isn't thick enough for you, mix 1 teaspoon cornstarch with 2 teaspoons cold water and gently stir into the sauce.)

4. Transfer the linguine and sauce to a large serving bowl. Dust with the Parmesan cheese and serve immediately.

Storage: *Refrigerate leftovers, tightly covered, for up to 2 days.*

PER SERVING: 365 calories; 21g protein; 6g total fat; 3g fiber; 52g carbohydrates; 32mg cholesterol; 358mg sodium

Main Dishes

BEEF

Chipotle Grilled New York Steaks

Grilled T-Bone Florentine

Grilled Mustard-Marinated Skirt Steak

Steak Diane

Chicken-Fried Steak

Cube Steak with Marinara Sauce

Swiss Steak

Veal Piccata

Mini Meat Loaves

Mexican Skillet Beef and Rice

PORK

Smothered Pork Chops

Pork Cutlets with Marsala Wine and Mushrooms

Slow Cooker Baby Back BBQ Ribs

CHICKEN

Jamaican Jerk Chicken with Mango Chutney

Barbecued Apricot-Mustard Chicken

Pan-Roasted Chicken Breasts with Apricot-Teriyaki Glaze

Bourbon-Orange Chicken

Chicken Parmesan

Chicken Cacciatore

Chicken Curry

Chicken Saltimbocca

Chicken Enchiladas

Lemon Chicken

FISH AND SEAFOOD

Shrimp Scampi

Shrimp, Sausage, and Pineapple Skewers

Shrimp and Grits

Grilled Teriyaki Tuna

Grilled Grouper with Ginger-Orange Glaze

Baked Red Snapper in Foil

Salmon en Papillote

Roasted Halibut on Mediterranean Vegetables

Salmon Simmered in Beer

VEGETARIAN

Mediterranean Pizza

Chipotle Grilled New York Steaks

MAKES: 4 SERVINGS   PREPARATION TIME: 5 MINUTES (PLUS 15 MINUTES STANDING TIME)
GRILLING TIME: 10 TO 15 MINUTES

If you like flavorful steaks, you'll love this easy recipe featuring chipotle chile powder, which adds heat, and herbed Montreal steak seasoning. Letting the steaks come to room temperature after you season them ensures that they will cook evenly and more quickly. Instead of grilling, you can broil the steaks for 4 to 5 minutes on each side, or to your preferred degree of doneness.

    4 New York strip steaks (about 4 ounces each)
    1 tablespoon Montreal steak seasoning or seasoning blend of choice
  ¼ teaspoon chipotle chile powder

1. Pat the steaks dry with paper towels. Combine the seasoning and chili powder and rub it on both sides of the steaks. Let the steaks stand at room temperature for 15 minutes (or proceed directly to grilling if time is short).

2. Place a barbecue rack about 6 inches away from the heat source. Preheat the grill to medium-high heat. Grill the steaks on one side for 4 to 5 minutes, until browned. Turn the meat over with tongs and cook on the other side, about 4 minutes more for rare, or 5 to 6 minutes more for medium-rare. To check for doneness, make a small cut in the thickest part. For longer cooking, move the steaks to a cooler part of the grill.

3. Transfer the steaks to a serving platter and allow to rest, covered with aluminum foil, for 5 minutes. Serve immediately.

Storage: Refrigerate leftovers, tightly wrapped, for up to 3 days.

PER SERVING: 250 calories; 16g protein; 20g total fat; 0g fiber; 0g carbohydrates; 63 mg cholesterol; 338mg sodium

Grilled T-Bone Florentine

MAKES: 4 SERVINGS   PREPARATION TIME: 5 MINUTES (PLUS 15 MINUTES STANDING TIME)
GRILLING TIME: 10 TO 15 MINUTES

Despite its romantic name, this dish—which originated in Florence, Italy (hence the name)—is quick to make, hearty, and satisfying. Rub the steaks with garlic first, then prepare the rest of your meal while they stand. You can also broil the steaks for 4 to 5 minutes on each side, or to your preferred degree of doneness.

  2 large garlic cloves, minced
  4 small T-bone steaks (about 4 ounces each)
  1 teaspoon salt, plus more to taste
  ½ teaspoon freshly ground black pepper, plus more to taste
  2 lemons, halved
  2 teaspoons olive oil

1. Rub the minced garlic over the steaks and sprinkle with the salt and pepper. Let the steaks stand for at least 15 minutes at room temperature.

2. Place a barbecue rack about 6 inches away from the heat source. Preheat the grill to medium-high heat. Grill the steaks on one side for 3 to 4 minutes, until browned. Turn the meat over with tongs and cook on the other side, about 3 minutes more for rare, or 4 minutes more for medium-rare. To check for doneness, make a small cut in the thickest part. For longer cooking, move the steaks to a cooler part of the grill. Transfer the steaks to a serving platter and allow to rest, covered with aluminum foil, for 5 minutes.

3. To serve, squeeze half a lemon over each steak, then drizzle with olive oil and serve immediately, adding additional salt and pepper if desired. (You may also remove the bones and cut the steaks into thin slices for serving instead.)

Storage: Refrigerate leftovers, tightly wrapped, for up to 3 days.

PER SERVING: 225 calories; 17g protein; 16g total fat; 0g fiber; 2g carbohydrates; 50mg cholesterol; 581mg sodium

Grilled Mustard-Marinated Skirt Steak

MAKES: 4 SERVINGS   PREPARATION TIME: 5 MINUTES
MARINATING TIME: 24 HOURS
GRILLING TIME: 15 TO 20 MINUTES (INCLUDES STANDING TIME)

Marinating this economical cut of meat for 24 hours is the secret to its marvelous flavor—then you can get it on the table in less than 20 minutes. It is very important to slice it on the diagonal (across the grain, not with the grain) to ensure that every bite is as tender as possible (see below). You can also broil the steak for 4 to 5 minutes on each side, or to your preferred degree of doneness.

¼ cup red wine vinegar
¼ cup lemon juice
2 tablespoons olive oil
2 tablespoons brown sugar
2 tablespoons Dijon mustard
1 large garlic clove, minced
1 teaspoon salt
2 teaspoons fresh oregano or 1 teaspoon dried
  Dash of hot pepper sauce
1 pound skirt steak

1. In a medium bowl, whisk together the vinegar, lemon juice, oil, brown sugar, mustard, garlic, salt, oregano, and hot pepper sauce until thoroughly combined. Pour into a heavy-duty, plastic food-storage bag. Add the skirt steak and marinate at least overnight, and preferably for 24 hours.

2. Place a barbecue rack about 6 inches away from the heat source. Preheat the grill to medium-high heat. Remove the steak from the marinade (discard marinade) and grill the steak on one side for 3 to 4 minutes. Turn the meat over with tongs and cook on the other side, about 3 minutes more for rare, or 4 minutes more for medium-rare. To check for doneness, make a small cut in the thickest part. For longer cooking, move the steak to a cooler part of the grill. Transfer the steak to a serving platter, cover with aluminum foil, and let rest for 5 minutes. Slice diagonally into ⅛-inch strips against the grain with a sharp knife or an electric knife and serve immediately.

Storage: Refrigerate leftovers, tightly wrapped, for up to 3 days.

PER SERVING: 300 calories; 22g protein; 19g total fat; Og fiber; 10g carbohydrates; 58mg cholesterol; 712mg sodium

SLICING MEAT AGAINST THE GRAIN

Flank steak and skirt steak are less tender cuts of meat. The first secret to tenderness is to slice off any membrane before cooking. Second, slice the cooked meat into very thin slices on the diagonal or bias, which means against the grain. Look for the lines on the cooked meat; they indicate the grain's direction. Then, holding a very sharp knife at a 45-degree angle to the meat, slice it as thinly as possible in a perpendicular direction to the grain. This breaks the meat fibers and makes it more tender.

Steak Diane

MAKES: 4 SERVINGS   PREPARATION TIME: 5 MINUTES
COOKING TIME: 15 TO 20 MINUTES

This classic restaurant dish is often flamed tableside in a dramatic performance. My version is much easier; in fact, you probably won't need a recipe the second or third time you make it. You can vary the ingredients, such as using more mushrooms or more lemon juice, depending on your tastes. It pairs nicely with Cannellini Beans with Wilted Spinach (page 93).

   4 filets mignon (about 4 ounces each)
   ½ teaspoon plus ⅛ teaspoon salt
   ½ teaspoon freshly ground black pepper
   2 tablespoons butter or buttery spread
   1 (8-ounce) can sliced mushrooms, drained
   2 tablespoons finely chopped green onion
   1 tablespoon brandy, or 1 teaspoon brandy extract (optional)
   1 tablespoon lemon juice
   2 teaspoons gluten-free Worcestershire sauce
   1 teaspoon Dijon mustard
   1 garlic clove, crushed
   2 tablespoons chopped fresh parsley

1. Sprinkle the steaks with ½ teaspoon of the salt and the pepper. Let stand while preparing the sauce.

2. In a large skillet, melt 1 tablespoon of the butter over medium heat. Add the mushrooms, green onion, brandy (if using), lemon juice, Worcestershire sauce, mustard, garlic, and the remaining ⅛ teaspoon salt, and cook, stirring, until the onions are tender, about 5 minutes. Stir in the parsley. Pour the sauce into a small saucepan, cover, and keep warm on a burner.

3. To cook the steaks: Melt the remaining 1 tablespoon butter in the skillet. Add the steaks and cook over medium-high heat until nicely browned on one side, 4 to 5 minutes. Turn the meat over with tongs and cook on the other side, about 4 minutes for rare, or 5 to 6 minutes for medium-rare. To check for doneness, make a small cut in the thickest part. Serve the steaks immediately with the mushroom sauce.

Storage: *Refrigerate leftovers, tightly wrapped, for up to 3 days.*

PER SERVING: 330 calories; 18g protein; 26g total fat; 1g fiber; 4g carbohydrates; 79mg cholesterol; 481mg sodium

Chicken-Fried Steak

MAKES: 4 SERVINGS   PREPARATION TIME: 10 MINUTES   FRYING TIME: 10 MINUTES

Served with mashed potatoes and green peas, this is classic comfort food. To save prep time, pound the steaks the night before so you can get them on the table more quickly.

- 1 cup Carol's Sorghum Blend (page 15)
- 1 cup finely crushed gluten-free savory crackers (about 25 crackers the size of saltines)
- 2 teaspoons gluten-free seasoned salt, or to taste
- ¼ teaspoon freshly ground black pepper
- ½ cup milk of choice
- 2 large eggs
- 4 cube steaks (about 4 ounces each)
- ¼ cup canola oil

1. In a shallow bowl, combine the sorghum blend, crackers, salt, and pepper. In another shallow bowl, whisk the milk and eggs together until all of the egg membrane is broken up and the mixture is very smooth.

2. Place the steaks between sheets of plastic wrap and use a meat mallet to pound them to ¼ to ⅓ inch thick. Dip the steaks first in the sorghum mixture, then in the egg mixture, and then in the sorghum mixture again. Lay on a cutting board.

3. In a large, heavy skillet, heat the oil over medium-high heat. Working in batches, fry the steaks until golden brown, 4 to 5 minutes per side, turning only once. If you turn them more than once, the coating will fall off. Transfer the steaks to a platter; cover with foil to keep warm while frying the remaining steaks. Serve immediately.

Storage: *Refrigerate leftovers, tightly wrapped, for up to 3 days.*

PER SERVING: 560 calories; 27g protein; 31g total fat; 3g fiber; 44g carbohydrates; 158mg cholesterol; 886mg sodium

Cube Steak with Marinara Sauce

MAKES: 4 SERVINGS   PREPARATION TIME: 2 MINUTES
FRYING TIME: 5 TO 10 MINUTES

This is one of my "fix-it-quick" recipes that I learned from a fellow
graduate student long ago, when we were severely time-challenged
and I had a husband and young son to feed when I got home from
classes. Cube steaks cook quickly, and store-bought marinara helps get
this dinner ready pronto.

- 1 tablespoon canola oil
- 4 cube steaks (about 4 ounces each)
- 1 teaspoon salt
- ½ teaspoon freshly ground black pepper
- 1 cup store-bought gluten-free marinara or spaghetti sauce
- ½ cup shredded mozzarella cheese or cheese alternative

1. In a large, heavy skillet, heat the oil over medium heat. Sprinkle
the steaks with the salt and pepper, add to the pan, and brown on
both sides, 1 to 2 minutes per side. To check for doneness, make a
small cut in the thickest part.

2. Top each steak with ¼ cup marinara sauce and 2 tablespoons
mozzarella cheese. Cover the skillet with a lid and cook over low
heat for 1 minute or until the cheese melts. Serve immediately.

Storage: Refrigerate leftovers, tightly wrapped, for up to 3 days.

PER SERVING: 340 calories; 26g protein; 23g total fat; 1g fiber; 6g carbohydrates;
83mg cholesterol; 910mg sodium

Swiss Steak

MAKES: 4 SERVINGS   PREPARATION TIME: 5 MINUTES
COOKING TIME: 20 TO 25 MINUTES

Most Swiss Steak recipes don't require smoked paprika, but I just love the robust flavor it lends to this dish (see below). To save time, blend together the sauce ingredients (tomatoes, broth, and seasonings) and chop the onion, garlic, and celery the night before. Refrigerate overnight so that all you have to do at dinnertime is sear the steaks and simmer the dish for 20 minutes.

- 1 pound beef top round, cut into 4 steaks
- 1 teaspoon salt
- ½ teaspoon freshly ground black pepper
- ½ cup cornstarch, plus 1 tablespoon for thickening sauce
- 2 tablespoons canola oil
- 1 large onion, thinly sliced
- 2 celery stalks, chopped
- 1 large garlic clove, minced
- 1 (14- to 15-ounce) can petite diced tomatoes, undrained
- 1 tablespoon tomato paste
- 2 teaspoons gluten-free Worcestershire sauce
- 1 teaspoon smoked paprika or regular paprika
- 2 teaspoons chopped fresh oregano or 1 teaspoon dried
- 1 (14- to 15-ounce) can or 1¾ cups gluten-free low-sodium beef broth
- 2 tablespoons chopped fresh parsley

SMOKED PAPRIKA

Most of the paprika sold in grocery stores is simply labeled "paprika" and is made of ground chile peppers. But if your recipe calls for "smoked paprika," look for that specific label. It indicates that the chile peppers have been smoked over a wood fire before being ground, which contributes a deep, woodsy flavor that is wonderful in a wide variety of savory dishes, including this steak.

1. Sprinkle both sides of the steaks with the salt and pepper. Place the ½ cup cornstarch in a shallow bowl. Dredge the steaks on both sides in the cornstarch.

2. In a Dutch oven or other deep, heavy pot with a tight-fitting lid, heat the oil over medium-high heat. Add the steaks, being careful not to overcrowd them or they will steam rather than sear. Cook until golden brown on both sides, about 2 minutes per side. Transfer the steaks to a plate.

3. Add the onion, celery, and garlic to the Dutch oven. Cook for 2 minutes or until the onion begins to soften. Add the tomatoes, tomato paste, Worcestershire sauce, paprika, oregano, and beef broth and stir to combine. Return the steaks to the pot. Cover and simmer over low heat for 15 to 20 minutes.

4. Transfer the steaks to a serving platter and cover with aluminum foil to keep warm. If the juices in the pot need thickening, stir the remaining 1 tablespoon cornstarch into 2 tablespoons cold water until smooth. Stir enough of the cornstarch mixture into the juices over medium-high heat until the juices thicken. Pour over the steaks and serve immediately, garnished with the parsley.

Storage: *Refrigerate leftovers, tightly wrapped, for up to 3 days.*

PER SERVING: 400 calories; 28g protein; 21g total fat; 2g fiber; 25g carbohydrates; 67mg cholesterol; 693mg sodium

Veal Piccata

MAKES: 4 SERVINGS   PREPARATION TIME: 10 MINUTES
COOKING TIME: 8 TO 10 MINUTES

This Italian-style dish featuring veal with a brightly flavored sauce of white wine, lemon juice, capers, and parsley comes together very quickly and requires your close attention because veal cooks so fast. Be sure to have all the other dishes in the meal ready to serve before you start cooking this entrée.

    4   veal cutlets (about 4 ounces each), pounded to ⅛-inch thickness
    1   teaspoon salt, or to taste
   ½   teaspoon freshly ground black pepper
   ½   cup cornstarch
  1½   tablespoons olive oil
    2   tablespoons butter or buttery spread
    1   cup dry white wine
   ¼   cup lemon juice
    1   garlic clove, chopped
    2   tablespoon capers, rinsed and drained
    1   tablespoon chopped fresh parsley, plus parsley sprigs for garnish

1. Sprinkle the veal with the salt and pepper. Place the cornstarch in a shallow bowl and dredge the veal in it, shaking to remove any excess.

2. In a large skillet, heat the oil over medium-high heat until hot. Add 1 tablespoon of the butter and, working quickly, cook the veal in batches until golden brown on both sides, about 1 minute per side. Transfer the veal to a plate and cover with aluminum foil to keep warm.

3. Add the wine to the pan and bring to a boil, scraping to loosen any browned bits from the bottom of the pan. When the wine has reduced by half, add the lemon juice, garlic, and capers and cook for 5 minutes, or until the sauce has thickened slightly. Whisk in the remaining 1 tablespoon butter and the chopped parsley. When the butter has melted, return the veal to the pan and cook until heated through and the sauce has thickened, about 1 minute. Serve immediately, garnished with parsley sprigs.

Storage: *Refrigerate leftovers, tightly wrapped, for up to 3 days.*

PER SERVING: 365 calories; 22g protein; 19g total fat; 0g fiber; 17g carbohydrates; 109mg cholesterol; 729mg sodium

Mini Meat Loaves

MAKES: 4 SERVINGS   PREPARATION TIME: 5 MINUTES
BAKING TIME: 20 TO 25 MINUTES

Meat loaf is one of America's best comfort foods, but it takes a while to bake in loaf form. Instead, put my "individual-muffin" version on the table in 30 minutes by using a muffin pan. Instead of ground beef, you may use ground pork or turkey—or a mixture.

- 1 cup store-bought gluten-free marinara or spaghetti sauce
- 1 large egg, beaten
- 1 cup gluten-free bread crumbs (see page 136)
- 1 tablespoon dried minced onion
- 2 teaspoons store-bought dried Italian seasoning
- ½ teaspoon salt
- ¼ teaspoon ground allspice
- ¼ teaspoon freshly ground black pepper
- 1 pound lean ground beef

1. Preheat the oven to 350°F. Generously grease a standard 12-cup nonstick muffin pan (gray, not black) or line with foil cupcake liners.

2. In a large bowl, combine ½ cup of the marinara sauce with the egg, bread crumbs, onion, Italian seasoning, salt, allspice, and black pepper. Mix with your hands or a spatula until well blended. Add the ground beef and mix thoroughly. (Or, put everything in a 1-gallon, heavy-duty, plastic food storage bag and massage until all the ingredients are well blended.) Divide the mixture among the 12 muffin cups and make a slight indentation in each with a teaspoon. Pour about 2 teaspoons of the remaining marinara sauce into each indentation.

3. Bake until the tops are nicely browned and an instant-read thermometer registers 160°F when inserted into the center, 20 to 25 minutes. Serve immediately.

Storage: *Refrigerate leftovers, tightly wrapped, for up to 3 days.*

PER SERVING: 525 calories; 23g protein; 33g total fat; 2g fiber; 34g carbohydrates; 143mg cholesterol; 616mg sodium

Mexican Skillet Beef and Rice

MAKES: 4 SERVINGS   PREPARATION TIME: 10 MINUTES
COOKING TIME: 10 MINUTES

This dish is for really busy nights when you want dinner on the table right away. Serve it with a tossed salad, along with corn tortillas wrapped in damp paper towels and heated gently in the microwave. This is a good way to use up leftover cooked brown rice that you've stored in the refrigerator or freezer. Or, quickly cook instant brown rice while browning the ground beef.

   8 ounces lean ground beef
   ¼ cup chopped onion or 1 tablespoon dried minced onion
   ½ cup water
  1½ tablespoons chili powder
   1 teaspoon chopped fresh oregano or ½ teaspoon dried
   ½ teaspoon ground cumin
   ¼ teaspoon salt
   1 cup cooked brown rice
   1 (14- to 15-ounce) can pinto beans or black beans, rinsed and drained
   1 (4-ounce) can diced green chiles
   2 medium plum tomatoes, seeded and chopped
   2 tablespoons chopped fresh cilantro

1. In a large skillet, cook the ground beef and onion over medium-high heat until browned, about 5 minutes, stirring to crumble the beef. The beef will be more flavorful if it is fully browned and all the liquid has evaporated.

2. Add the water, chili powder, oregano, cumin, and salt and stir to combine. Stir in the rice, beans, and chiles and heat to serving temperature, about 5 minutes. Top with the chopped tomatoes; garnish with the chopped cilantro. Serve immediately, right from the skillet.

Storage: *Refrigerate leftovers, tightly wrapped, for up to 3 days.*

PER SERVING: 520 calories; 29g protein; 8g total fat; 28g fiber; 85g carbohydrates; 21mg cholesterol; 234mg sodium

Smothered Pork Chops

MAKES: 4 SERVINGS   PREPARATION TIME: 5 MINUTES
COOKING TIME: 20 TO 25 MINUTES

Smothered pork chops are an all-American comfort food. Here, they are covered in a delicious onion- and- garlic-based gravy which is thickened and made creamy with buttermilk (see right). Once the chops are simmering, they require no attention from you—freeing you to prepare the rest of the meal while they cook.

    4 boneless pork chops (about 4 ounces each), about ½ inch thick
 ½ cup cornstarch, plus 2 tablespoons for the gravy
    1 teaspoon onion powder
 ¼ teaspoon cayenne pepper
 ¼ teaspoon garlic powder
    1 teaspoon salt, plus more to taste
 ¼ teaspoon freshly ground black pepper, plus more to taste
 ¼ cup canola oil
    1 cup gluten-free low-sodium chicken broth
 ½ cup buttermilk or plain kefir
       Chopped fresh parsley, for garnish

1. Pat the pork chops dry with paper towels. In a shallow bowl, whisk together the ½ cup cornstarch with the onion powder, cayenne, garlic powder, salt, and pepper. Dip the chops into the mixture.

2. In a large, heavy skillet, heat the oil over medium heat. Lay the pork chops in the skillet in a single layer, taking care not to crowd them. If they are too close together, they will steam rather than brown. Fry for 7 to 10 minutes on each side, until golden brown.

3. Remove the pork chops from the skillet. Add ¾ cup of the chicken broth and cook over medium heat until the liquid is reduced slightly. Stir 2 tablespoons of the remaining cornstarch mixture into the remaining ¼ cup chicken broth and add to the skillet. Cook over medium heat until slightly thickened. Reduce the heat to low and stir in the buttermilk.

4. Return the pork chops to the skillet, spooning the sauce over them. Cover and simmer for 5 minutes or until the pork is cooked through. Season with additional salt and pepper, if desired, and serve immediately, garnished with chopped parsley.

Storage: Refrigerate leftovers, tightly wrapped, for up to 3 days.

PER SERVING: 415 calories; 24g protein; 19g total fat; 0g fiber; 36g carbohydrates; 52mg cholesterol; 741mg sodium

HOMEMADE BUTTERMILK SUBSTITUTES

Buttermilk does wonderful things for gluten-free baking, but unfortunately it is made from cow's milk, which makes it inappropriate for dairy-sensitive people. However, you can make your own dairy-free buttermilk by adding 1 tablespoon of vinegar or lemon juice to 1 cup of milk of your choice. Let stand for a few minutes to thicken slightly; do not stir. Or, if you can eat dairy products, use plain kefir (a fermented milk drink made from cow's milk), which is similar in texture and acidity to buttermilk. Kefir is usually quite thick, so use ¾ cup kefir and ¼ cup water to thin it down in a recipe that calls for 1 cup buttermilk.

Pork Cutlets with Marsala Wine and Mushrooms

MAKES: 4 SERVINGS   PREPARATION TIME: 5 MINUTES
COOKING TIME: 12 TO 15 MINUTES

Marsala wine, from the Sicilian city of the same name, is often used in Italian cooking. This classic dish is delicious served over Easy Soft Polenta (page 86), with the pan juices drizzled on top. Serve it on weekdays when you're pressed for time, but it's also a wonderful weekend dish for guests.

  4 pork cutlets (4 ounces each)
  ½ teaspoon salt
  ½ teaspoon freshly ground black pepper
  1 tablespoon olive oil
  ¼ cup dry Marsala wine
  1 teaspoon balsamic vinegar
  1 (8-ounce) can sliced mushrooms, undrained
  1 garlic clove, minced
  1 tablespoon chopped fresh rosemary
  4 cups hot cooked soft polenta (see page 86)

1. Pat the cutlets dry and sprinkle with the salt and pepper.

2. In a large, heavy skillet, heat the oil over medium heat. Add the cutlets and cook until lightly browned on one side, 3 to 4 minutes. Turn and cook until the other side is browned and crispy, 2 to 3 minutes more.

3. Add the wine, vinegar, mushrooms, garlic, and rosemary. Simmer gently for 3 to 5 minutes or until the cutlets are cooked through and the juices reduce slightly. Transfer the cutlets to a serving platter and pour the reduced juices and mushrooms on top. Serve immediately over hot cooked polenta.

Storage: *Refrigerate leftovers, tightly wrapped, for up to 3 days.*

PER SERVING: 475 calories; 24g protein; 15g total fat; 8g fiber; 57g carbohydrates; 56mg cholesterol; 320mg sodium

Slow Cooker Baby Back BBQ Ribs

MAKES: 6 SERVINGS   PREPARATION TIME: 10 MINUTES
COOKING TIME: 7 TO 9 HOURS

Ribs don't have to be cooked on a barbecue grill to be delicious. This isn't a 30-minute recipe, per se, but you can enjoy saucy, savory ribs anytime by using a slow cooker. It takes a while to cook, but your prep time is only about 10 minutes. Store-bought sauce and barbecue seasoning are big time-savers.

- 4 pounds baby back pork ribs
- 4 tablespoons McCormick Grill Mates barbecue seasoning
- 1 yellow onion, sliced
- ½ cup water
- 1½ cups store-bought gluten-free barbecue sauce, plus more for serving

1. Spray the inside of a 6-quart slow cooker crock with cooking spray.

2. Sprinkle the ribs with the barbecue seasoning and cut the slabs into 4-inch pieces. In the slow cooker, layer or wedge the ribs in between slices of onion. Pour the water around the edges of the slow cooker.

3. Cover and cook on Low for 6 to 8 hours, until the ribs are tender when pierced with a fork.

4. Remove the ribs and onions from the cooker and discard the liquid. Return the onions to the slow cooker and layer or wedge the ribs on top of the onions, pouring some of the barbecue sauce over each rack of ribs as you layer them. Cover and cook on Low for 1 hour longer to let the sauce flavor the ribs. Serve immediately, with extra sauce if desired.

Storage: Refrigerate leftovers, tightly wrapped, for up to 3 days.

PER SERVING: 590 calories; 33g protein; 45g total fat; 1g fiber; 10g carbohydrates; 146mg cholesterol; 653mg sodium

CHICKEN

Jamaican Jerk Chicken with Mango Chutney

MAKES: 4 SERVINGS   PREPARATION TIME: 5 MINUTES
MARINATING TIME: OVERNIGHT   COOKING TIME: 15 TO 20 MINUTES

Jerk, a style of cooking native to Jamaica, involves marinating the meat in seasonings for vibrant flavor. Although this is a quick dish to cook, it is best when the chicken marinates overnight, so plan ahead. These flavors are enhanced by store-bought sweet mango chutney. Chicken legs (drumsticks) are smaller than other chicken parts, allowing the flavorful marinade to penetrate better—and they cook more quickly than larger pieces. You can also broil the chicken, following Step 2 to test for doneness.

- 3 tablespoons McCormick Jamaican jerk seasoning
- 2 tablespoons canola oil
- 1 tablespoon gluten-free low-sodium soy sauce
- 1 tablespoon cider vinegar
- 1 tablespoon lime juice
- 12 chicken legs (about 1¼ pounds)
- 1 teaspoon salt
- ½ teaspoon freshly ground black pepper
- 1 cup store-bought mango chutney

1. Combine the jerk seasoning with the oil, soy sauce, vinegar, and lime juice in a heavy-duty, plastic resealable bag. Add the chicken legs, tossing to make sure all the pieces are coated with the marinade. Refrigerate overnight or all day.

2. Place a barbecue grill 6 inches away from the heat source. Preheat the grill to medium heat. Remove the chicken legs from the marinade and shake off any excess. Sprinkle the chicken legs with the salt and pepper. Cook on the grill until browned, 5 to 7 minutes, basting occasionally with the reserved marinade. Turn and continue cooking until the chicken legs are browned all over and the juice is no longer pink when the center of the thickest part of the legs is cut, or an instant-read thermometer registers 165°F when inserted into the thickest part. Serve immediately with the chutney.

Storage: *Refrigerate leftovers, tightly covered, for up to 3 days.*

PER SERVING: 415 calories; 19g protein; 20g total fat; 2g fiber; 40g carbohydrates; 86mg cholesterol; 780mg sodium

Barbecued Apricot-Mustard Chicken

MAKES: 4 SERVINGS (2 PIECES EACH)   PREPARATION TIME: 5 MINUTES
COOKING TIME: 15 TO 20 MINUTES

Partially cooking the chicken pieces in the microwave on low power before grilling them shortens the grill time and lessens the chance of them burning, because the chicken spends less time on the high-heat grill. This precooking technique is a real time-saver that you can use for other grilled dishes, too. You can also broil the chicken, following Step 3 to test for doneness.

CHICKEN

- 8 chicken pieces, preferably legs or thighs (about 1¼ pounds)
- 1 teaspoon salt
- ½ teaspoon freshly ground black pepper

APRICOT-MUSTARD GLAZE

- ⅓ cup apricot jam or preserves
- ¼ cup cider vinegar
- 2 tablespoons Dijon mustard
- 1 tablespoon canola oil
- 1 garlic clove, minced
- ½ teaspoon onion powder
- ½ teaspoon salt
- ¼ teaspoon chili powder
- ¼ teaspoon freshly ground black pepper

1. PREPARE THE CHICKEN: Place the chicken in a single layer on a microwave-safe plate and sprinkle with the salt and pepper. Cover with waxed paper and partially cook by microwaving on High power for about 10 minutes. Let stand. Place a barbecue grill about 6 inches away from the heat source. Preheat the grill to medium-low heat.

2. MAKE THE GLAZE: In a small bowl, stir together all of the ingredients until smooth.

3. Transfer the chicken to the heated grill. Cook skin side down until the skin starts to brown, about 5 minutes. Turn the chicken skin

CONTINUED ON PAGE 130

CONTINUED FROM PAGE 129

side up and continue to cook, brushing the chicken with the glaze periodically until it's done, another to 5 to 10 minutes depending on the size of the chicken pieces and the intensity of the heat. The chicken is done when the juice is no longer pink when the center of the thickest part of the legs is cut, or an instant-read thermometer registers 165°F when inserted into the thickest part. If chicken starts to brown too quickly, turn the heat down to low and watch carefully.

Storage: *Refrigerate leftovers, tightly covered, for up to 3 days.*

PER SERVING: 300 calories; 19g protein; 16g total fat; 1g fiber; 19g carbohydrates; 86mg cholesterol; 986mg sodium

Pan-Roasted Chicken Breasts with Apricot-Teriyaki Glaze

MAKES: 4 SERVINGS   PREPARATION TIME: 5 MINUTES
COOKING TIME: 25 TO 30 MINUTES

Sweet apricot jam and savory soy sauce make a delightful glaze for these chicken breasts. Pan roasting involves browning the chicken breasts in a skillet, then transferring them—skillet and all—to finish cooking in a preheated oven. It roasts untended while you complete the remainder of the meal.

   4 boneless, skinless chicken breast halves (about 1 pound)
   ¼ teaspoon salt
   ¼ teaspoon freshly ground black pepper
   2 tablespoons canola oil
   ⅔ cup store-bought gluten-free teriyaki sauce
   ⅔ cup apricot jam
   ¼ cup sliced almonds
   1 tablespoon sesame seeds
   1 tablespoon chopped fresh parsley

1. Place a rack in the middle of the oven. Preheat the oven to 350°F. With a meat mallet, pound the chicken breasts to a ½-inch thickness between two sheets of plastic wrap. Sprinkle with the salt and pepper.

2. In a large, heavy ovenproof skillet, heat the oil over medium-high heat. Brown the chicken breasts, about 5 minutes per side depending on size, or until the juice is no longer pink when the center of the thickest part is cut.

3. Meanwhile, while the chicken is browning, mix together the teriyaki sauce and apricot jam until well blended. When the chicken is browned, pour the sauce over the chicken and bake in the oven, uncovered, for 15 to 20 minutes or until the chicken is cooked through and an instant-read thermometer registers 165°F when inserted into the thickest part. The sauce will thicken into a glaze as the chicken bakes.

4. During the last 5 minutes of baking, spoon the glaze over the chicken breasts and then sprinkle the almonds and sesame seeds on top. Remove the skillet from the oven and transfer the chicken to a serving platter, spooning the glaze around the breasts on the platter. Serve garnished with the parsley.

Storage: *Refrigerate leftovers, tightly covered, for up to 3 days.*

PER SERVING: 415 calories; 30g protein; 16g total fat; 2g fiber; 41g carbohydrates; 66mg cholesterol; 883mg sodium

Bourbon-Orange Chicken

MAKES: 4 SERVINGS   PREPARATION TIME: 10 MINUTES
FRYING TIME: 10 TO 15 MINUTES

Bourbon's remarkable flavor complements the orange in this dish and lends depth and complexity. If you would rather not use bourbon (see below), use the same amount of orange juice.

- 4 boneless, skinless chicken breast halves (about 1 pound)
- 1 teaspoon salt
- ½ teaspoon freshly ground black pepper
- ¼ cup cornstarch
- 2 tablespoons olive oil
- ½ cup orange juice concentrate, thawed
- 2 garlic cloves, minced
- 1 green onion (including green top), finely chopped
- ½ cup bourbon or orange juice
- 1 tablespoon champagne vinegar
- 2 tablespoons chopped fresh parsley and/or chives

1. Cut each chicken breast half into 2 pieces. Sprinkle the chicken with the salt and pepper and place in a single layer in a 1-gallon heavy-duty, plastic food storage bag. With a meat mallet, pound the chicken to about a ½-inch thickness. In a shallow bowl, dredge the chicken in 3 tablespoons of the cornstarch.

2. In a large skillet, heat the oil and cook the chicken over medium-high heat until lightly browned and crisp, 4 to 5 minutes per side, or until the juice is no longer pink when the center of the thickest part is cut. Transfer the chicken to a serving platter and cover with aluminum foil to keep it warm. Remove the skillet from the heat.

3. Mix the remaining 1 tablespoon cornstarch into the orange juice concentrate until smooth. Add to the skillet along with the garlic, green onion, bourbon, and vinegar. Return the skillet to the stove over low heat and stir for 2 minutes or until the sauce thickens. Pour the sauce over the chicken and serve immediately, garnished with the parsley.

Storage: Refrigerate leftovers, tightly covered, for up to 3 days.

PER SERVING: 345 calories; 27g protein; 8g total fat; 1g fiber; 22g carbohydrates; 66mg cholesterol; 611mg sodium

ALCOHOLIC BEVERAGES FOR A GLUTEN-FREE DIET?

Distilled liquors such as bourbon, whiskey, and vodka are gluten-free because—even if they are made with gluten grains—the gluten peptides cannot survive the distillation process. However, fermented drinks such as beer or ale contain gluten because the wheat or barley used in their processing survives the fermentation process. Wines, hard ciders, and after-dinner liqueurs are not distilled but are generally gluten-free, unless gluten-containing flavors or ingredients are added.

Chicken Parmesan

MAKES: 4 SERVINGS   PREPARATION TIME: 10 MINUTES
COOKING TIME: 12 TO 15 MINUTES

The easy-to-make Parmesan-Herb Blend makes this dish very tasty—with very little effort. The blend makes about ½ cup, so keep the leftover blend in the fridge to use on other meats. Pounding the chicken breasts to an even thickness with a meat mallet makes them cook a lot faster and can be done the night before. Keep store-bought marinara sauce on hand for dishes such as this one.

PARMESAN-HERB BLEND

   3 tablespoons grated Parmesan cheese or soy Parmesan
   ¼ cup chopped fresh basil or 2 tablespoons dried
   4 teaspoons chopped fresh thyme or 2 teaspoons dried
   ½ teaspoon garlic powder
   ¼ teaspoon salt

CHICKEN

   4 boneless, skinless chicken breast halves (about 1 pound)
   ½ teaspoon salt
   ½ teaspoon freshly ground black pepper
   ½ cup gluten-free bread crumbs (see page 136)
   2 tablespoons cornstarch
   2 tablespoons canola oil
   ½ cup store-bought gluten-free marinara or spaghetti sauce
   ½ cup shredded mozzarella cheese or cheese alternative

1. MAKE THE HERB BLEND: In a small bowl, combine all of the ingredients until thoroughly blended.

2. PREPARE THE CHICKEN: With a meat mallet, lightly pound the chicken breasts to about a ½-inch thickness between sheets of plastic wrap. Sprinkle with the salt and pepper. In a shallow dish or plate, combine the bread crumbs, ¼ cup of the herb blend, and the cornstarch. Dip both sides of the chicken breasts in the crumb mixture, pressing it onto the chicken with your fingers.

3. In a large, heavy skillet, heat the oil over medium-high heat. Cook the chicken breasts until lightly browned on both sides and the juices run clear, 7 to 10 minutes. Turn the heat to low. While the chicken breasts are still in the skillet, top each with 2 tablespoons marinara sauce and 2 tablespoons mozzarella cheese. Cover the skillet with a lid or aluminum foil and cook for 2 minutes more or until the marinara sauce is heated through and the cheese melts. Serve immediately.

CONTINUED ON PAGE 136

CONTINUED FROM PAGE 135

Storage: *Refrigerate leftovers, tightly covered, for up to 3 days.*

PER SERVING: 335 calories; 33g protein; 14g total fat; 1g fiber; 17g carbohydrates; 81mg cholesterol; 746mg sodium

Homemade Bread Crumbs

MAKES: 2 CUPS

4 cups gluten-free bread of choice, torn into small pieces

Place the bread in a food processor and pulse on and off until the crumbs reach the desired consistency. For Italian bread crumbs, toss with 1 teaspoon onion powder and 4 teaspoons dried Italian seasoning, or to taste. Store tightly covered in the refrigerator for up to 2 weeks or in the freezer for up to 3 months.

Chicken Cacciatore

MAKES: 4 SERVINGS   PREPARATION TIME: 10 MINUTES
COOKING TIME: 25 TO 30 MINUTES

Cacciatore means "hunter" in Italian, so this is a hunter's stew. The delicious aroma wafting from your kitchen while this dish cooks is incredibly inviting on cold, wintry nights. If you have homemade marinara in your freezer, this is a great use for it; store-bought marinara sauce shortens the cooking time considerably. If you have time, replace the canned mushrooms with 1 cup sliced fresh mushrooms instead.

   2 tablespoons olive oil
   4 boneless, skinless chicken breast halves (about 1 pound)
   1 (8-ounce) can chopped mushroom pieces, drained
   1 small onion, finely diced
   1 garlic clove, minced
   2 cups store-bought gluten-free marinara or spaghetti sauce
   2 tablespoons capers, rinsed and drained (optional)
   8 ounces gluten-free penne or spiral pasta

1. In a Dutch oven or other deep, heavy pot with a tight-fitting lid, heat the olive oil over medium-high heat. Add the chicken breasts and cook until golden brown on all sides, about 5 minutes per side. Transfer to a plate. Add the mushrooms and onion to the skillet and cook until the onion is translucent, about 3 minutes. Add the garlic, marinara sauce, and capers to the skillet and stir until blended.

2. Return the chicken breasts to the Dutch oven and bring to a boil. Reduce the heat to low and simmer, covered, for 15 minutes.

3. While the cacciatore simmers, cook the pasta in salted boiling water according to the package directions until done. Serve immediately with the cacciatore.

Storage: Refrigerate leftovers, tightly covered, for up to 3 days.

PER SERVING: 480 calories; 36g protein; 12g total fat; 5g fiber; 55g carbohydrates; 66mg cholesterol; 632mg sodium

Chicken Curry

MAKES: 4 SERVINGS   PREPARATION TIME: 10 MINUTES
COOKING TIME: 20 MINUTES

This may seem like a lot of measuring, but it's worth it! Curry is a
flavorful dish that requires many spices to achieve its marvelous flavor.
For more heat, use ½ teaspoon cayenne. Beyond that, you're on your
own! Be sure to have hot, cooked rice ready, or quickly cook instant
rice while the curry simmers.

    2 tablespoons canola oil
    1 pound cubed white chicken meat (about 1¾ cups)
    1 cup canned petite diced tomatoes, undrained
  ½ teaspoon ground mustard
  ¼ teaspoon cayenne pepper, or to taste
  ¼ teaspoon ground cumin
  ¼ teaspoon ground turmeric
  ¼ teaspoon curry powder
  ¼ teaspoon salt
  ⅛ teaspoon ground cloves
  ¾ cup canned coconut milk
    4 cups hot, cooked white basmati rice
    2 tablespoons chopped fresh cilantro

1. In a large skillet, heat the oil over medium-high heat. Cook the
chicken until darkly browned on all sides, 5 to 7 minutes.

2. Stir in the tomatoes, mustard, cayenne, cumin, turmeric, curry
powder, salt, cloves, and coconut milk until blended. Reduce the heat
to low and simmer for 10 minutes or until the chicken is completely
cooked through and the juices reduce down slightly. Serve over hot
cooked rice, garnished with the cilantro.

Storage: Refrigerate leftovers, tightly covered, for up to 3 days.

PER SERVING: 570 calories; 41g protein; 23g total fat; 4g fiber; 50g carbohydrates;
96mg cholesterol; 233mg sodium

Chicken Saltimbocca

MAKES: 4 SERVINGS   PREPARATION TIME: 10 MINUTES
BAKING TIME: 25 TO 30 MINUTES

Saltimbocca is Italian for "jumps in the mouth," and this dish is so named because of its full flavor. It will be easier to assemble if you buy thin-sliced chicken breasts, but regular size will work, too. If they are particularly thick, slice them in half. You just have to pound them more to get the ⅛-inch thickness.

> 4 thin-sliced boneless, skinless chicken breast halves (about 1 pound)
> 2 thin slices prosciutto (about 1 ounce total), cut in half lengthwise to make 4 slices
> 2 large garlic cloves, minced
> 1 tablespoon dried rubbed sage
> ½ teaspoon freshly ground black pepper
> 1 tablespoon butter or buttery spread
> 1 tablespoon olive oil
> 4 thin slices (about 4 ounces total) provolone cheese or cheese alternative
> Grated zest and juice of 1 lemon
> 2 tablespoons chopped fresh parsley or 1 tablespoon dried

1. Place a rack in the middle of the oven. Preheat the oven to 325°F. With a meat mallet, pound each chicken breast to a ⅛-inch thickness between two sheets of plastic wrap. Remove the plastic wrap and lay each breast on a slice of prosciutto. Rub the minced garlic, sage, and pepper on the top side of the chicken. Fold the chicken and prosciutto in half (with the prosciutto inside the fold) and secure with a toothpick at the open end.

2. In a nonstick ovenproof skillet, heat the butter and olive oil over medium heat. Place each chicken breast in the skillet and cook until it is brown on the bottom, 3 to 5 minutes. Turn and brown on the other side, 3 to 5 minutes more. Cover and place the skillet in the preheated oven to finish cooking, 12 to 15 minutes, depending on the size and thickness of the chicken breasts, until the juice is no longer pink when the center of the thickest part is cut.

3. Place a slice of cheese on each breast and return it to the oven for a few minutes, until the cheese melts. Remove from the oven, drizzle the lemon juice over the chicken breasts, and garnish with the lemon zest and parsley. Serve immediately.

Storage: Refrigerate leftovers, tightly covered, for up to 3 days.

PER SERVING: 300 calories; 36g protein; 16g total fat; 0g fiber; 3g carbohydrates; 97mg cholesterol; 509mg sodium

Chicken Enchiladas

MAKES: 4 SERVINGS   PREPARATION TIME: 10 MINUTES
BAKING TIME: 20 TO 25 MINUTES

For many of us in the Southwest, enchiladas are a weekly mainstay—in one form or another. They are highly versatile, lending themselves to a wide variety of fillings beyond chicken. Store-bought gluten-free red enchilada sauce and leftover cooked chicken save precious time.

>   2 cups grated reduced-fat cheddar cheese or cheese alternative, plus
>   2 tablespoons for sprinkling
>   2 cups cooked shredded chicken (see page 142)
>   2 tablespoons olive oil
>   8 gluten-free corn tortillas
> 2½ cups store-bought gluten-free enchilada sauce
>   ½ cup sour cream or sour cream alternative
>   ½ cup chopped green onions

1. Place a rack in the middle of the oven. Preheat the oven to 350°F. Coat a 7×11-inch baking dish with cooking spray.

2. In a medium bowl, combine 2 cups of the cheddar cheese with the chicken. Set aside.

3. In a small skillet, heat the oil over medium heat. Using tongs, dip the tortillas into the hot oil—one at a time—to soften them, and then drain on paper towels.

4. Place the enchilada sauce in a wide, shallow bowl. Dip a tortilla in the sauce and lay it on a plate. Fill with ¼ cup of the chicken filling and 3 tablespoons enchilada sauce, and roll up. Place the enchilada seam side down in the baking dish. Repeat with the remaining tortillas. Top the enchiladas with the remaining sauce and sprinkle with the remaining 2 tablespoons cheddar cheese.

5. Bake for 20 to 25 minutes, or until the sauce is bubbly and the cheese melts. Top with the sour cream and green onions and serve immediately.

CONTINUED ON PAGE 142

CONTINUED FROM PAGE 141

Storage: *Refrigerate leftovers, tightly covered, for up to 3 days.*

PER SERVING: 615 calories; 43g protein; 32g total fat; 8g fiber; 43g carbohydrates; 120mg cholesterol; 671mg sodium

HOW TO SHRED MEAT

Meat is easier to shred when it's hot. Right after cooking, let it stand for 15 minutes, wrapped in aluminum foil, to reabsorb its juices. Then unwrap it and place on a flat surface, such as a cutting board. Holding a fork in each hand, place the first fork into the meat aligned with the grain and hold it steady. Then place the second fork into the meat and pull it away from the first fork. Repeat this process until all of the meat is shredded into small pieces.

Lemon Chicken

MAKES: 4 SERVINGS   PREPARATION TIME: 10 MINUTES
COOKING TIME: 15 MINUTES

This dish, often found in Chinese restaurants, is super-easy to make at home. Just brown the chicken breasts and then create a simple, lemony pan sauce to pour over them. Be sure to have cooked rice on hand to save time and you will have a meal that is better than any take-out version.

- 4 boneless, skinless chicken breast halves (about 1 pound)
- ½ cup cornstarch, plus 2 tablespoons for thickening sauce
- ½ teaspoon salt
- 2 tablespoons canola oil
- 1 teaspoon ground ginger
- 1 cup gluten-free low-sodium chicken broth
- 2 tablespoons honey or agave nectar
- 2 tablespoons lemon juice
- 1 tablespoon cider vinegar
- 1 teaspoon grated lemon zest
- 2 tablespoons dried chives, or ½ cup green onions finely chopped diagonally
- 4 cups hot cooked basmati (or other) rice

1. Pat the chicken breasts dry with paper towels. With a meat mallet, pound the chicken between sheets of plastic wrap to flatten just slightly.

2. In a medium bowl, whisk together the ½ cup cornstarch and the salt. Dip each chicken breast in the cornstarch mixture to coat thoroughly.

3. In a large, heavy skillet, heat the oil over medium-high heat. Cook the chicken for 5 minutes on each side, depending on size, or until nicely browned and the juice is no longer pink when the center of the thickest part is cut. Remove from the skillet and cover with aluminum foil to keep warm.

4. Stir the remaining 2 tablespoons cornstarch and the ginger into ¼ cup of the chicken broth until smooth. Add to the skillet, along with the remaining ¾ cup chicken broth and honey. Cook over medium heat, stirring frequently, until the mixture thickens and comes to a boil. Remove from the heat. Stir in the lemon juice, vinegar, and lemon zest.

5. Cut each chicken breast into 4 slices, slightly on the diagonal. Arrange on a serving platter and pour the sauce over the chicken. Sprinkle with the chives and serve immediately over the hot cooked rice.

Storage: *Refrigerate leftovers, tightly covered, for up to 3 days.*

PER SERVING: 530 calories; 34g protein; 10g total fat; 4g fiber; 74g carbohydrates; 66mg cholesterol; 474mg sodium

Shrimp Scampi

MAKES: 4 SERVINGS   PREPARATION TIME: 5 MINUTES
COOKING TIME: UNDER 5 MINUTES

Light yet marvelously flavorful, this is one of the quickest recipes to prepare because shrimp cooks so fast. Have all the other dishes in the meal prepared because this one will be ready to serve in no time. It is relatively low in calories and naturally gluten-free, and did I mention marvelously flavorful? I cook the shrimp in a butter-oil mix so it doesn't burn as easily as it might if cooked in butter only. Olive oil also improves the nutrition profile of the dish.

- 1 tablespoon butter or buttery spread
- 1 tablespoon extra-virgin olive oil
- 2 pounds large shrimp, peeled and deveined
- 4 garlic cloves, minced
- ½ cup dry white wine
- ½ teaspoon salt
- ¼ teaspoon crushed red pepper
  Grated zest and juice of 1 lemon, plus more for garnish
- ¼ cup chopped fresh parsley
  Salt and freshly ground black pepper to taste

1. In a large, heavy skillet, heat half of the butter and half of the oil over medium heat. Add half of the shrimp and cook for 1 minute. Transfer the shrimp to a plate, and cook the remaining shrimp in the remaining butter and oil for 1 minute, then transfer to the plate. Add the garlic to the skillet and sauté for 1 minute. Add the wine, salt, and red pepper and simmer for 30 seconds. Return all of the shrimp to the skillet. Add the lemon zest and lemon juice and cook for 30 seconds more, tossing to coat the shrimp thoroughly with the juices.

2. Serve immediately in the skillet with a squeeze of lemon juice, a sprinkle of lemon zest and parsley, and a dusting of salt and pepper.

Storage: Refrigerate leftover shrimp scampi, tightly covered, for up to 1 day.

PER SERVING: 325 calories; 46g protein; 10g total fat; 0g fiber; 5g carbohydrates; 353mg cholesterol; 607mg sodium

Shrimp, Sausage, and Pineapple Skewers

MAKES: 4 SERVINGS (2 SKEWERS EACH)   PREPARATION TIME: 5 MINUTES
GRILLING TIME: 5 MINUTES

Shrimp skewers are easy to make and cook quickly because shrimp and sausage chunks are small. Andouille sausage is highly flavorful, and the sweet pineapple contrasts deliciously with the spicy chili glaze. Be sure to soak wooden skewers in water for 20 to 30 minutes to prevent them from catching fire on the grill.

- 1 pound extra-large shrimp, peeled and deveined, with tails on
- 4 gluten-free andouille sausage links, cut into 1-inch chunks
- 1 (14-ounce) can pineapple chunks, well drained
- 1 medium red bell pepper, seeded and cut into 1-inch chunks
- 1 medium green bell pepper, seeded and cut into 1-inch chunks
- ½ cup chili sauce
- 2 teaspoons lemon juice
- ¼ teaspoon honey or agave nectar
- Dash of hot pepper sauce, or to taste

1. Thread all of the shrimp together on skewers (3 or 4 to a skewer), so they will cook at their own speed and won't overcook. Then thread the sausage chunks, pineapple chunks, and bell pepper chunks alternately on the remaining skewers.

2. In a small bowl, whisk together the chili sauce, lemon juice, honey, and hot pepper sauce until blended.

3. Place a barbecue grill about 6 inches away from the heat source. Preheat the grill to medium-high heat. Place the skewers on the grill and cook until the shrimp are pink and opaque, 4 to 5 minutes, and the other items are heated through, generously brushing the skewers with the chili sauce during the last minute of cooking. Remove the food from the skewers and serve immediately.

Storage: Refrigerate leftovers, tightly wrapped in aluminum foil, for up to 2 days.

PER SERVING: 345 calories; 27g protein; 13g total fat; 3g fiber; 28g carbohydrates; 192mg cholesterol; 365mg sodium

Shrimp and Grits

MAKES: 4 SERVINGS   PREPARATION TIME: 10 MINUTES
COOKING TIME: 20 MINUTES

With my microwave-style grits, this classic Southern dish is super-quick (no standing at the stovetop, stirring, stirring, stirring...). For the prettiest yellow grits, be sure to use light-colored chicken or vegetable broth (or water).

GRITS
- 3 cups gluten-free low-sodium chicken broth (or vegetable broth)
- ¾ cup Bob's Red Mill gluten-free polenta/corn grits
- 1 bay leaf
- ¼ teaspoon salt
- ¼ teaspoon freshly ground black pepper
- 2 tablespoons butter or buttery spread
- 1 tablespoon extra-virgin olive oil

SHRIMP AND SAUSAGE
- 2 tablespoons butter or buttery spread
- 1 tablespoon olive oil
- 1 small onion, finely chopped
- 1 link gluten-free andouille sausage, cut into ¼-inch slices
- 1 pound medium shrimp, peeled and deveined
- 1 garlic clove, minced
- 2 tablespoons chopped fresh parsley
- 2 tablespoons grated Parmesan cheese or soy Parmesan

1. **MAKE THE GRITS:** In a large, microwave-safe bowl (I use an 8-cup Pyrex measuring cup, which is large enough to avoid boil-overs), whisk together all of the ingredients. Lay a sheet of waxed paper over the bowl and cook in the microwave on High power in 10-minute increments, whisking between each increment, to reach the desired consistency. Cooking times may vary depending on your microwave; mine takes two 10-minute increments, for a total of 20 minutes.

2. **WHILE THE GRITS COOK, MAKE THE SHRIMP AND SAUSAGE:** In a medium, heavy skillet, heat the butter and olive oil over medium heat. Cook the onion and sausage until the onion is tender and the sausage is browned on both sides. Add the garlic and shrimp and cook for 4 to 5 minutes, until the shrimp turn pink. Stir the shrimp mixture into the grits, remove the bay leaf, and serve hot, garnished with the parsley and Parmesan cheese.

Storage: *Refrigerate leftovers, tightly sealed, for up to 2 days.*

PER SERVING: 470 calories; 36g protein; 24g total fat; 4g fiber; 27g carbohydrates; 210mg cholesterol; 787mg sodium

GRITS OR POLENTA?

The difference between grits and polenta can be confusing, especially because they look so much alike. Both polenta and grits are made from stone-ground cornmeal, but Southerners use the term grits while Italians use the term polenta. Some experts also claim that the two are ground from different types of corn and have different textures, particularly in degree of coarseness. When cooked, finely ground grits are smoother and mushier while more coarsely ground grits give a heartier, more toothsome texture. Of the two, I prefer the more toothsome bite, so I use Bob's Red Mill brand coarse-ground gluten-free grits, which are bright yellow and labeled with both terms— polenta and corn grits.

Grilled Teriyaki Tuna

MAKES: 4 SERVINGS   PREPARATION TIME: 5 MINUTES
MARINATING TIME: 20 MINUTES   GRILLING TIME: 10 TO 15 MINUTES

This is a great dish for busy nights when you want a special meal, but plan ahead to marinate the tuna. Assemble the marinade in the plastic bag the night before, eliminating an extra dish to wash—then marinate the tuna shortly before grilling. For options, you can broil the tuna or use halibut fillets, if you like.

- ½ cup store-bought gluten-free teriyaki sauce
- 2 tablespoons toasted sesame oil
- 2 tablespoons brown sugar
- 1 tablespoon grated lime zest
- 1 teaspoon ground ginger
- ⅛ teaspoon crushed red pepper
- 4 yellowfin tuna fillets (4 ounces each)
- 1 teaspoon sesame seeds, toasted

1. Stir together the teriyaki sauce, oil, brown sugar, lime zest, ginger, and crushed red pepper in a heavy-duty, plastic food storage bag, seal tightly, and refrigerate overnight. Right before dinner, add the tuna and shake to coat the tuna thoroughly. Refrigerate for 20 minutes while you prepare the rest of the meal.

2. Place a barbecue grill about 6 inches away from the heat source. Preheat the grill to medium-high heat. Remove the tuna from the bag and reserve the marinade. Grill the tuna until it reaches the desired degree of doneness, 8 to 10 minutes, depending on the thickness of the fillet, or until the fish is just barely opaque when cut in the thickest part.

3. In a small saucepan, bring the reserved marinade to a boil and let boil for 2 minutes. Transfer to a pitcher to serve as a sauce. Remove the tuna from the grill and arrange it on a serving platter. Drizzle the sauce over the tuna and sprinkle with the sesame seeds. Serve immediately.

Storage: *Refrigerate leftovers, tightly covered, for up to 2 days.*

PER SERVING: 285 calories; 29g protein; 13g total fat; 0g fiber; 13g carbohydrates; 43mg cholesterol; 547mg sodium

Grilled Grouper with Ginger-Orange Glaze

MAKES: 4 SERVINGS   PREPARATION TIME: 5 MINUTES
MARINATING TIME: 20 MINUTES   GRILLING TIME: 10 TO 15 MINUTES

Grouper is a thick, hearty white fish, but you may substitute thick red snapper or salmon if you wish. If you don't want to grill this dish, broil it instead. Watch closely, because it cooks quickly.

- 3 tablespoons gluten-free low-sodium soy sauce
- 3 tablespoons Dijon mustard
- 3 tablespoons orange juice concentrate, thawed
- 1 tablespoon grated fresh ginger
- 4 grouper fillets (about 4 ounces each)
- 1 orange, cut into wedges

1. In a heavy-duty, plastic food storage bag, combine the soy sauce, mustard, orange juice concentrate, and ginger. Add the grouper and shake to coat the grouper thoroughly. Refrigerate for 20 minutes. Remove the grouper from the bag and transfer the marinade to a small saucepan.

2. Place a barbecue grill about 6 inches away from the heat source. Preheat the grill to medium-high heat. Cook the fish to the desired degree of doneness, 8 to 10 minutes, or until the crumbs are golden and the fish is just barely opaque when cut in the thickest part. Cooking time will vary with the thickness of the fish.

3. Meanwhile, while the fish grills, bring the marinade to a boil over medium heat and let boil for 3 minutes. The marinade will reduce down slightly. Pour a little of the marinade over the cooked fish, and serve hot with the orange wedges.

Storage: Refrigerate leftovers, tightly covered, for up to 2 days.

PER SERVING: 290 calories; 52g protein; 3g total fat; 1g fiber; 11g carbohydrates; 96 mg cholesterol; 729mg sodium

Baked Red Snapper in Foil

MAKES: 4 SERVINGS   PREPARATION TIME: 10 MINUTES   BAKING TIME: 15 MINUTES

This super-easy dish can be prepared the night before you need it, then baked just before serving dinner the next night. Once you get the hang of it, you can vary the ingredients as you wish. Instead of spinach, use thin asparagus spears; the red snapper might be replaced with sole; or the red bell pepper can be replaced with sliced tomatoes. Use your imagination!

- ⅓ cup (roughly 5 tablespoons) butter or buttery spread, at room temperature
- 2 tablespoons chopped fresh thyme
- 2 tablespoons chopped fresh chives
- 1 tablespoon lemon juice
- 1 tablespoon grated lemon zest
- 2 dashes of hot pepper sauce, or ⅛ teaspoon cayenne pepper
- 1 teaspoon celery salt
- ½ teaspoon lemon pepper
- 4 cups baby spinach
- 1 small red bell pepper, seeded, cored, and sliced into ⅛-inch strips
- 4 red snapper fillets (4 ounces each), 1 inch thick
- 8 lemon slices
- 1 lemon, cut into quarters

1. Place a rack in the middle of the oven. Preheat the oven to 425°F. In a small bowl, blend the butter with the thyme, chives, lemon juice, lemon zest, hot pepper sauce, celery salt, and lemon pepper.

2. Arrange four 12-inch square pieces of aluminum foil on the countertop, and place 1 cup spinach and one-quarter of the sliced red pepper in the center of each square. Place a red snapper fillet on top. Top each fillet with the butter mixture, dividing evenly. Place 2 lemon slices on each fillet. Wrap the foil around the fillet, pleating the top and twisting the ends securely to avoid leakage. Arrange the packets on a rimmed 9×13-inch baking sheet. You may refrigerate the packets overnight or all day at this point.

3. Bake for 12 to 15 minutes, or until the fish flakes easily with a fork. Transfer the packets to serving plates, roll back the foil to each side to form a decorative opening (beware of the steam), and serve immediately with the lemon wedges.

Storage: *Refrigerate leftovers, tightly covered, for up to 1 day.*

PER SERVING: 240 calories; 19g protein; 17g total fat; 2g fiber; 4g carbohydrates; 73mg cholesterol; 523mg sodium

Salmon en Papillote

MAKES: 4 SERVINGS   PREPARATION TIME: 10 MINUTES   BAKING TIME: 15 MINUTES

En papillote loosely translates from French as "wrapped in packets." Cooking food wrapped in parchment (or aluminum foil) helps seal in and blend the flavors and juices. It is easy to entertain with these little packets because you can prepare them the night before—leaving you more time for other last-minute details.

- 4 salmon fillets (about 4 ounces each)
- 1 small carrot, peeled and julienned
- 1 small leek, white part only, root end cut off, sliced and rinsed thoroughly to remove grit
- 1 teaspoon grated fresh ginger
- 1 garlic clove, minced
- 1 teaspoon salt
- ½ teaspoon freshly ground black pepper
- 2 teaspoons toasted sesame oil
- 2 teaspoons extra-virgin olive oil

1. Place a rack in the middle of the oven. Preheat the oven to 425°F. Arrange four 12-inch square pieces of parchment paper on a flat surface. Place a salmon fillet on each piece.

2. In a small bowl, combine the carrot, leek, ginger, garlic, ½ teaspoon of the salt, and ¼ teaspoon of the pepper. Place one-quarter of this mixture on each piece of salmon. Top each piece with the remaining salt and pepper. Drizzle with the sesame oil and olive oil. Bring two edges of the parchment paper together and crimp or fold together to seal tightly. Twist the ends together to seal tightly. You may refrigerate the packets overnight or all day at this point.

3. Place the packets on a 9×13-inch rimmed baking sheet and coat them with cooking spray.

4. Bake for 12 to 15 minutes. The packets will puff up and brown. Remove from the oven and place each packet on a serving plate. Slowly cut open the packets with scissors to allow steam to release gently. Serve immediately.

Storage: *Refrigerate leftovers, tightly covered, for up to 1 day.*

PER SERVING: 195 calories; 23g protein; 9g total fat; 1g fiber; 5g carbohydrates; 59mg cholesterol; 620mg sodium

Roasted Halibut on Mediterranean Vegetables

MAKES: 4 SERVINGS   PREPARATION TIME: 10 MINUTES
ROASTING TIME: 20 MINUTES

This one-pot dish is so simple yet delicious, with its warm
Mediterranean flavors. You just put everything in the baking dish and
let the oven do the work. It may seem like a lot of spinach, but it will
shrink down considerably during the roasting process.

1 (10-ounce) bag baby spinach
1 (6.5-ounce) jar marinated artichokes, drained
2 garlic cloves, minced
1 cup yellow or red grape tomatoes, or a mix of both, halved
4 halibut fillets (about 4 ounces each)
2 tablespoons extra-virgin olive oil
2 tablespoons dry white wine
1 teaspoon store-bought dried Mediterranean herb seasoning
½ teaspoon salt
¼ teaspoon freshly ground black pepper or lemon pepper

1. Place a rack in the middle of the oven. Preheat the oven to
400°F. In a large bowl, toss the spinach, artichokes, and garlic
together and then place on the bottom of a 2-quart ovenproof
baking dish. Place the tomatoes around the edges.

2. Arrange the halibut fillets on top of the vegetables; drizzle them
with the olive oil and wine, and sprinkle with the herb seasoning, salt,
and pepper. Cover tightly with a lid or aluminum foil.

3. Roast for 10 minutes, then remove the lid and roast for 8 to
10 minutes more, depending on the thickness of the fish, or until
the fish is just barely opaque when cut in the thickest part. Serve
immediately.

Storage: Refrigerate leftovers, tightly covered, for up to 2 days.

PER SERVING: 260 calories; 27g protein; 12g total fat; 4g fiber; 8g carbohydrates;
36mg cholesterol; 520mg sodium

Salmon Simmered in Beer

MAKES: 4 SERVINGS   **PREPARATION TIME:** 5 MINUTES
GRILLING TIME: 12 TO 15 MINUTES

There are many brands and styles of gluten-free beer, so choose your favorite and enjoy salmon cooked in this flavorful liquid. If you don't want to use the grill, simmer the salmon on the stove in a covered skillet instead.

- 1 pound salmon fillet or 4 (4-ounce) salmon steaks
- 2 tablespoons brown sugar
- 2 teaspoons onion powder
- 1 teaspoon salt
- ½ teaspoon seafood seasoning
- ½ teaspoon freshly ground black pepper
- 1 (12-ounce) bottle gluten-free beer
- 1 lemon, quartered

1. Place a barbecue grill about 6 inches away from the heat source. Preheat the grill to medium-high heat. Place the salmon in a heavy-duty aluminum-foil baking pan that is large enough to hold all of the salmon in a single layer. In a small bowl, combine the sugar, onion powder, salt, seafood seasoning, and pepper until thoroughly blended. Sprinkle around and over the salmon. Pour the beer around the salmon and cover the pan tightly with aluminum foil.

2. Cook the salmon on the grill until the fish is just barely opaque when cut in the thickest part or it flakes easily with a fork, about 8 to 12 minutes. Spoon the beer over the salmon, then remove the salmon from the pan and serve immediately with the lemon wedges.

Storage: *Refrigerate leftovers, tightly covered, for up to 2 days.*

PER SERVING: 200 calories; 23g protein; 4g total fat; 0g fiber; 13g carbohydrates; 59mg cholesterol; 788mg sodium

Mediterranean Pizza

MAKES: 8 SERVINGS **PREPARATION TIME:** 10 MINUTES
BAKING TIME: 30 TO 35 MINUTES

This recipe is a favorite! Start with the pizza crust, then use any toppings you like. A flour shaker (available at kitchen stores and online) is useful for evenly dusting the dough with flour to prevent it from sticking to your hands. For additional time-saving tips, see Ideas for Quicker Pizza on page 34.

BASIL PIZZA SAUCE

   1 (8-ounce) can tomato sauce
   2 teaspoons fresh basil or 1 teaspoon dried
   2 teaspoons fresh parsley or 1 teaspoon dried
  ¼ teaspoon fennel seeds
  ¼ teaspoon garlic powder
  ⅛ teaspoon salt
  ⅛ teaspoon sugar

PIZZA CRUST

   1 tablespoon active dry yeast
2½ teaspoons sugar
  ¾ cup milk of choice, warmed to 110°F
  ⅔ cup potato starch
  ½ cup Carol's Sorghum Blend (page 15), plus more for dusting
   1 teaspoon xanthan gum
   1 teaspoon store-bought dried Italian seasoning
   1 teaspoon onion powder
  ½ teaspoon salt
   1 tablespoon olive oil
   2 teaspoons cider vinegar
     Shortening, for greasing pizza pan

TOPPING

   1 (11-ounce) jar marinated artichokes, drained
   1 cup sliced red, yellow, or green bell peppers, sautéed
  ½ cup chopped sun-dried tomatoes
  ½ cup sliced black olives
   6 slices smoked mozzarella cheese or cheese alternative
   1 tablespoon olive oil

CONTINUED ON PAGE 158

CONTINUED FROM PAGE 157

1. MAKE THE SAUCE: Combine all of the ingredients in a small saucepan. Simmer for 15 minutes; set aside.

2. MAKE THE CRUST: Place a rack in the bottom position and another in the middle position of the oven. Preheat the oven to 425°F. In a small bowl, dissolve the yeast and sugar in the warm milk. Let foam for 5 minutes. In a food processor, blend the yeast mixture, potato starch, sorghum blend, xanthan gum, Italian seasoning, onion powder, salt, oil, and vinegar until a ball forms. The dough will be very soft.

3. Generously grease a 12-inch nonstick pizza pan (gray, not black) with shortening. Do not use cooking spray—it makes it harder to shape the dough. Place the dough on the prepared pan and liberally dust the dough with flour blend; then press the dough into the pan with your hands, continuing to dust the dough with flour to prevent sticking as needed. The smoother the dough, the smoother the baked crust will be. Make the edges a bit thicker to contain the toppings.

4. Bake the pizza crust on the bottom rack for 15 minutes, or until the crust begins to brown on the bottom.

5. Remove the crust from the oven; brush it with the sauce and arrange the artichokes, peppers, tomatoes, and olives on the sauce. Sprinkle the cheese over the top. Place the pizza pan on the middle rack and bake for 15 to 20 minutes, until the cheese is nicely browned. Remove the pizza from the oven and let stand for 5 minutes.

6. Brush the rim of the crust with the olive oil before cutting into 6 slices. Serve immediately.

Storage: *Refrigerate leftovers, wrapped in aluminum foil, overnight. Eat cold the next day or reheat on a baking sheet in a 300°F oven.*

PER SLICE: 240 calories; 9g protein; 10g total fat; 5g fiber; 32g carbohydrates; 20mg cholesterol; 620mg sodium

Desserts

FRUIT DESSERTS
Berries in Gelatin
Grilled Fruit
Fresh Figs with Goat Cheese and Honey
Apple Crisp with Granola
Cherry Clafouti

CAKES, CHEESECAKES, COOKIES, AND BARS
Flourless Chocolate Cupcakes
Vanilla Cupcakes
Chocolate Brownies
White Chocolate, Apricot, and Almond Balls
Chocolate Refrigerator Cookies
No-Cook Chocolate Cheesecakes

PUDDINGS
Vanilla Pudding
Chocolate Pudding
Superfast Polenta Pudding
Black Forest Trifle
Chocolate Mousse

Berries in Gelatin

MAKES: 6 SERVINGS PREPARATION TIME: 5 MINUTES CHILLING TIME: OVERNIGHT

Serve this easy, make-ahead dessert in your prettiest glassware and your guests will be impressed—both at its beauty and at its wonderful lightness. Gelatin is both a retro-popular dessert and an ingredient that chefs experiment with. Feel free to play with it yourself; for example, try a sophisticated option of soaking the gelatin in white wine or sparkling wine instead of the juice, or showcase more exotic fruit like pomegranate arils or lingonberries. In-season fruit is best, but try to use at least three different colors for the prettiest effect. Glass serving dishes are best because they showcase the fruit's lovely colors. And, this naturally gluten-free dessert is a lovely way to get more fruit into your diet.

- 2 tablespoons unflavored powdered gelatin
- 4 cups white grape juice (1 cup chilled)
- 1 cup canned mandarin oranges, drained
- ½ cup fresh blueberries
- ½ cup fresh raspberries
  Whipped cream or whipped topping, for garnish (optional)
  Fresh mint leaves, for garnish (optional)

1. In a large bowl, stir the gelatin into the 1 cup cold white grape juice. Heat the remaining 3 cups grape juice in a medium saucepan until it simmers.

2. Add the hot white grape juice to the cold juice-gelatin mixture, stirring thoroughly until the gelatin is dissolved.

3. Chill the gelatin in the refrigerator for 45 to 60 minutes, until it just begins to set (it will be the texture of raw egg whites). Stir in the fruit until it is thoroughly distributed. Transfer the mixture to 6 glass cups or serving bowls. Chill all day or overnight. Serve chilled, garnished with whipped cream and mint leaves, if using.

Storage: *Refrigerate leftovers, tightly covered, for up to 1 day.*

PER SERVING: 160 calories; 1g protein; 0g total fat; 2g fiber; 39g carbohydrates; 0mg cholesterol; 27mg sodium

Grilled Fruit

MAKES: 4 SERVINGS   PREPARATION TIME: 2 MINUTES
GRILLING TIME: 5 TO 10 MINUTES, DEPENDING ON FRUIT

Grilled fruit is one of the easiest, fastest, and most rewarding of desserts—especially when the grill is already hot from cooking dinner. (Make sure to clean the grate so any savory flavoring is gone.)

The heat caramelizes natural sugars and heightens flavor, transforming fruit into a sweet, delicious, and nutritious dessert. Peaches, plums, and pears work very well, but pineapple, nectarines, and apricots are also good choices. This is a light, nutritious finishing touch after a big meal.

- **4 peaches, plums, or pears**
- **4 teaspoons canola or olive oil**
- **½ cup plain yogurt, whipped cream, whipped topping, or ice cream**
- **Honey, for drizzling**
- **¼ cup chopped walnuts, pecans, or pistachios, for garnish**
- **Fresh mint leaves, for garnish (optional)**

1. Preheat the grill to medium-high heat. On a cutting board, cut the fruit in half and remove the pits. Place the fruit cut side up on the board, and use a silicone pastry brush to coat the cut sides with the oil.

2. Grill the fruit, cut side down, until it is warm and grill marks are discernible on the cut side. Arrange 2 fruit halves on each dessert plate or in a wide glass goblet. Top each half with 1 tablespoon of yogurt, a drizzle of honey, and a sprinkle of the nuts. Serve immediately, garnished with mint leaves, if using.

Storage: *Refrigerate grilled fruit (without the yogurt, nuts, honey, or mint), tightly covered, for up to 1 day.*

PER SERVING: 125 calories; 3g protein; 10g total fat; 1g fiber; 6g carbohydrates; 4mg cholesterol; 15mg sodium

Fresh Figs with Goat Cheese and Honey

MAKES: 4 SERVINGS   PREPARATION TIME: 5 MINUTES

This super-easy but oh-so-healthy dessert combines fresh Black Mission figs (or whatever variety you have), a salty cheese such as Parmigiano-Reggiano, and good-quality honey—plus, if you dare, a slight dusting of freshly ground black pepper, which offers a surprisingly pleasant contrast to the sweetness of the figs and honey. If you have time, grilling the figs makes this dish even more spectacular. Figs are naturally healthy and lend variety—plus fiber and nutrients—to a gluten-free diet.

> **4** slices or shavings Parmigiano-Reggiano cheese or 8 wedges Daiya Havarti-style wedge cheese alternative
> **8** ripe but firm Black Mission figs, halved lengthwise
> **¼** cup honey or agave nectar
> Freshly ground black pepper, for garnish (optional)
> Fresh mint leaves, for garnish (optional)

1. Place a slice of cheese on four serving plates or in four glasses. Place 2 figs, cut side up, on the cheese.

2. Drizzle the honey on the figs, sprinkle lightly with black pepper (if using), and garnish with mint (if using). Serve at room temperature.

Storage: Though best eaten right away, the dessert can be refrigerated, tightly covered, for up to 1 day.

PER SERVING: 175 calories; 4g protein; 2g total fat; 4g fiber; 38g carbohydrates; 6mg cholesterol; 134mg sodium

Apple Crisp with Granola

MAKES: 4 SERVINGS   PREPARATION TIME: 10 MINUTES   BAKING TIME: 20 MINUTES

A perfect, simple, not-too-sweet dessert when the weather turns brisk and apples are abundant. Precooking the sliced apples in the microwave and using store-bought granola make this dessert superfast. You can even buy pre-sliced apples for greater time savings. Granny Smith apples hold their shape but take longer to cook; McIntosh or Jonathan apples are wonderfully flavorful in the fall. If you prefer a sweeter dessert, add more brown sugar to the apples, use a sweeter granola, or both.

    4 cups thinly sliced apples (4 large Gala, Granny Smith, or your choice)
    2 tablespoons raisins
    2 tablespoons brown sugar, or more to taste
    2 tablespoons cornstarch
    ½ teaspoon ground cinnamon
    ¼ teaspoon salt
    2 tablespoons butter or buttery spread, at room temperature
    2 tablespoons lemon juice
    1½ cups Udi's Naked Granola*

1. Place a rack in the middle of the oven. Preheat the oven to 375°F. Generously grease an 8-inch square microwave-safe glass baking dish.

2. In a medium bowl, toss the apples with the raisins, sugar, cornstarch, cinnamon, and salt until well blended. Add the butter and lemon juice to the bowl and mix thoroughly.

3. Place the pan of apple filling in the microwave and cover with waxed paper. Microwave on High power for 5 minutes to soften the apples. (You may also cook this apple mixture for 5 minutes, stirring occasionally, in a saucepan over medium heat on the stovetop.) Scatter the granola evenly over the apples and coat the granola with cooking spray.

4. Bake for 15 to 20 minutes, until the granola is lightly browned and the apples are tender. Cool the apple crisp in the pan for 10 minutes on a wire rack. Serve slightly warm.

Storage: Refrigerate leftovers, tightly covered, for up to 2 days.

* Check with your physician to make sure gluten-free oats are right for your diet.

PER SERVING: 170 calories; 0g protein; 6g total fat; 3g fiber; 31g carbohydrates; 16mg cholesterol; 138mg sodium

Cherry Clafouti

MAKES: 6 SERVINGS   PREPARATION TIME: 10 MINUTES
BAKING TIME: 25 TO 30 MINUTES

Clafouti (clah-FOO-tee) is a French dessert of fruit topped with a batter that bakes up like a combination of custard and pancake. It is an excellent dessert for busy cooks because it is so easy, it always works, and it is delicious. Plus, you can assemble clafouti ingredients in the ramekins ahead of time and refrigerate, then bake while eating dinner.

FRUIT

2 cups pitted canned Bing cherries, drained
1 tablespoon sugar
1 tablespoon cherry brandy (optional)
1 teaspoon pure almond extract

BATTER

3 large eggs, at room temperature
¼ cup sugar
½ cup Carol's Sorghum Blend (page 15)
½ cup milk of choice
1 teaspoon pure vanilla extract
1 teaspoon pure almond extract
¼ teaspoon salt
1 tablespoon sliced almonds
1 tablespoon powdered sugar

1. Place a rack in the middle of the oven. Preheat the oven to 350°F. Generously grease 6 ramekins, each 3½ to 4 inches in diameter.

2. PREPARE THE FRUIT: In a medium bowl, toss together the cherries, sugar, brandy (if using), and almond extract until well blended. Divide evenly among the ramekins.

3. MAKE THE BATTER: In a blender, combine the eggs, 3 tablespoons of the sugar, sorghum blend, milk, vanilla, almond extract, and salt until smooth. Pour evenly over the cherries. Sprinkle with the almonds and the remaining 1 tablespoon sugar.

4. Bake for 25 to 30 minutes or until the top is firm to the touch. Cool for 10 minutes on a wire rack before serving. Serve slightly warm, dusted with the powdered sugar.

Storage: *Refrigerate leftovers, tightly covered, for up to 1 day.*

PER SERVING: 180 calories; 5g protein; 4g total fat; 1g fiber; 30g carbohydrates; 109mg cholesterol; 42mg sodium

✳ Flourless Chocolate Cupcakes

MAKES: 12 CUPCAKES **PREPARATION TIME:** 5 MINUTES
BAKING TIME: 20 TO 25 MINUTES

Flourless cupcakes use ground nuts as the base and are extremely quick to assemble in a food processor. They also bake faster than standard-size cakes. Instead of the simple dusting of powdered sugar, you can top them as you like, with your favorite icing and decorations. These cupcakes are my go-to choice for gluten-free, dairy-free guests, but you can also use the batter for a 9-inch round cake (see the variation). Feel free to use the same amount of ground walnuts or pecans instead of the almonds, if you prefer. For best results, make sure the eggs are at room temperature.

- 2 cups almond flour/meal or 2 cups whole almonds
- 3/4 cup packed brown sugar
- 1/2 cup unsweetened cocoa powder (use either natural or Dutch-processed)
- 4 large eggs, at room temperature
- 1/2 cup canola oil
- 1 teaspoon pure vanilla extract
- 1/2 teaspoon salt
- 2 tablespoons powdered sugar

1. Place a rack in the middle of the oven. Preheat the oven to 350°F. Line a standard 12-cup nonstick muffin pan (gray, not black) with liners.

2. Place the almond meal in a food processor. (If using whole almonds, grind the nuts to a fine, meal-like texture.) Add the brown sugar, cocoa, eggs, oil, vanilla, and salt and process for 30 to 40 seconds. Scrape down the side of the bowl with a spatula and process for another 30 seconds or until the mixture is thoroughly blended. Divide the batter evenly among the muffin cups, using about 1/4 cup batter for each cupcake.

3. Bake for 20 to 25 minutes, until a toothpick inserted into the center of a cupcake comes out clean. Cool the cupcakes for 15 minutes in the pan on a wire rack, then transfer them to the wire rack to cool completely. Dust with powdered sugar before serving.

CONTINUED ON PAGE 170

CONTINUED FROM PAGE 169

Storage: *Store leftovers at room temperature, tightly covered, for up to 3 days.*

PER CUPCAKE: 390 calories; 10g protein; 31g total fat; 3g fiber; 22g carbohydrates; 62mg cholesterol; 117mg sodium

LAYER CAKE: Bake in a 9-inch nonstick springform pan (gray, not black) lined with parchment paper until a tester inserted into the center comes out clean, 35 to 40 minutes. Cool the cake in the pan for 15 minutes on a wire rack. Gently run a knife around the edge of the pan to loosen the cake. Invert the cake onto a serving plate, discard the paper, and let the cake cool completely.

ALMOND MEAL/FLOUR

Almond flour is sometimes called almond meal, but although the two work similarly in recipes, they do not look the same. Almond flour is ground from blanched almonds, which removes the skins and produces light-colored flour. Almond meal is ground from whole almonds, so the skins make the flour a darker color and consequently, the baked goods a bit darker as well. Bob's Red Mill grinds a version with the skins on and labels it as Natural Almond Flour. Almond flour and almond meal taste the same so you can use them interchangeably in this recipe. If you can't find either of them, grind whole almonds in your food processor to as fine a texture as possible without turning them into almond butter.

Vanilla Cupcakes

MAKES: 12 CUPCAKES PREPARATION TIME: 10 MINUTES
BAKING TIME: 20 TO 25 MINUTES

This basic vanilla cake batter can be baked as cupcakes or as a double-layer cake (see the variation), making it highly versatile. Of course, cupcakes bake more quickly. Frost with your favorite icing, decorate them as you like, or cut them in half horizontally for strawberry shortcake. These cupcakes are lighter in color when you use brown rice flour instead of the sorghum in Carol's Sorghum Blend.

½ cup butter or buttery spread, at room temperature
1¼ cups sugar
2 large eggs, at room temperature
2 cups Carol's Sorghum Blend (page 15)
2 teaspoons baking powder
1 teaspoon xanthan gum
½ teaspoon salt
⅛ teaspoon baking soda
¾ cup water, at room temperature
1 tablespoon grated lemon zest (optional)
1 teaspoon pure vanilla extract

1. Place a rack in the middle of the oven. Preheat the oven to 350°F. Line a standard 12-cup nonstick muffin pan (gray, not black) with liners.

2. In a medium bowl, beat the butter and sugar with an electric mixer on medium speed until well blended, about 3 minutes. Beat in the eggs, one at a time, until thick and lemon colored, about 2 minutes.

3. In another medium bowl, whisk together the sorghum blend, baking powder, xanthan gum, salt, and baking soda until well blended. In a small bowl, mix together the water, lemon zest (if using), and vanilla. Gradually beat the flour mixture into the egg mixture on low speed, alternating with the water mixture and beginning and ending with the flour mixture, until the batter thickens slightly, about 1 minute. Divide the batter evenly among the muffin cups, using about ¼ cup batter for each cupcake.

CONTINUED ON PAGE 172

CONTINUED FROM PAGE 171

4. Bake for 20 to 25 minutes, until the tops are firm and a toothpick inserted into the center of a cupcake comes out clean. Let the cupcakes cool for 15 minutes in the pan on a wire rack, then transfer them to the wire rack to cool completely.

Storage: *Store leftovers at room temperature, tightly covered, for up to 2 days.*

PER CUPCAKE: 240 calories; 2g protein; 9g total fat; 1g fiber; 40g carbohydrates; 52mg cholesterol; 194mg sodium

VANILLA LAYER CAKES: Generously grease two 9-inch round nonstick cake pans (gray, not black). Line the bottoms with parchment paper and grease again; set aside. Prepare the batter as directed and spread evenly in the pans (a scant 2 cups batter per pan). Bake until the cakes start to pull away from the edges of the pan and a toothpick inserted in the center comes out clean, about 25 to 30 minutes. Let the cakes cool in the pans for 15 minutes on a wire rack. Gently run a knife around the edge of the pan to loosen the cakes. Invert the cakes onto serving plates, discard the paper, and cool the cakes completely.

Chocolate Brownies

MAKES: 16 BROWNIES   PREPARATION TIME: 5 MINUTES   BAKING TIME: 20 MINUTES

Two kinds of chocolate assure fudgy decadence. Use leftovers as the basis for brownie sundaes by simply adding a scoop of ice cream, fudge sauce, and a maraschino cherry; or bake these in advance for the Black Forest Trifle (page 184).

- 3 ounces gluten-free semisweet baking chocolate, melted
- ⅓ cup canola oil
- ¾ cup packed brown sugar
- 2 large eggs, at room temperature
- 1 teaspoon pure vanilla extract
- 1 cup Carol's Sorghum Blend (page 15)
- ½ cup unsweetened natural cocoa powder (not Dutch-processed)
- 1 teaspoon xanthan gum
- ½ teaspoon baking powder
- ½ teaspoon salt
- ¼ cup very hot water or brewed coffee
- ¼ cup chopped walnuts

1. Preheat the oven to 350°F. Generously grease an 8-inch square glass baking dish for soft brownies or a nonstick baking pan (gray, not black) for crispier edges.

2. In a medium bowl, combine the melted chocolate with the oil and beat with an electric mixer on low speed until smooth, about 20 seconds. Beat in the brown sugar, eggs, and vanilla until thoroughly blended. Add the sorghum blend, cocoa, xanthan gum, baking powder, and salt and beat just until thoroughly blended. Blend in the hot water, then stir in the walnuts. Transfer the batter to the prepared pan and smooth the top with a wet spatula.

3. Bake for 20 minutes, or until the edges are firm but the center still appears wet. Don't overbake. Remove from the oven and let cool on a wire rack for 20 minutes. The brownies will firm up as they cool. Cut into 16 squares and serve at room temperature.

Storage: *Store leftovers at room temperature, tightly covered, for up to 3 days.*

PER BROWNIE: 160 calories; 2g protein; 8g total fat; 1g fiber; 22g carbohydrates; 23mg cholesterol; 94mg sodium

White Chocolate, Apricot, and Almond Balls

MAKES: 24 BALLS   PREPARATION TIME: 10 MINUTES

Serve these bite-size treats during the holidays or at dinner parties in little foil or paper candy liners. Their small size and rich, satisfying flavor make them ideal for when you want just a little something sweet, not an entire dessert. A food processor makes the prep superfast. You can replace the white chocolate with dark chocolate, if you wish.

        1 cup whole almonds
      2/3 cup powdered sugar
        2 cups dried apricots (about 12 ounces)
        2 tablespoons light or dark rum or orange juice
        2 teaspoons grated orange zest
        1 teaspoon pure vanilla extract
     3½ ounces white chocolate chips (or a 3.5-ounce bar white chocolate,
           chopped or broken into ¼-inch chunks)

1. In a food processor, process the almonds and powdered sugar until the almonds are very finely ground. Add the apricots and pulse until the apricots are very finely chopped.

2. Add the rum, orange zest, vanilla, and white chocolate chips and pulse until the mixture is just blended. With lightly oiled hands, roll and compress the dough into 24 balls, each 1 inch in diameter. Refrigerate for at least 1 hour to firm up. Serve in foil or paper candy liners.

Storage: Store leftovers, tightly covered, for up to 2 days in the refrigerator or for up to 1 month in the freezer.

PER BALL: 130 calories; 3g protein; 6g total fat; 2g fiber; 17g carbohydrates; 0mg cholesterol; 8mg sodium

✺ Chocolate Refrigerator Cookies

MAKES: 48 COOKIES   PREPARATION TIME: 10 MINUTES   CHILLING TIME: 2 HOURS
BAKING TIME: 10 TO 12 MINUTES

Refrigerator cookies come together in two basic steps: First, make the dough, and chill or freeze it. Next, bake as needed when you want. By planning ahead, you can have cookies in about 15 minutes.

  21 ounces gluten-free bittersweet chocolate chips (at least 60% cacao)
   5 tablespoons (about ⅓ cup) butter or buttery spread
   3 large eggs
   1 cup sugar
  ½ teaspoon pure vanilla extract
  ½ cup sorghum flour
  ¼ teaspoon baking soda
  ¼ teaspoon xanthan gum
  ¼ teaspoon salt
   1 cup finely chopped walnuts

1. In a medium microwave-safe bowl, heat 9 ounces of the chocolate chips with the butter in the microwave on Low power for 1 to 2 minutes, or until melted. Stir until well blended.

2. In a large bowl, beat the eggs, sugar, and vanilla with an electric mixer on low speed until thick, about 1 minute. In a small bowl, whisk together the flour, baking soda, xanthan gum, and salt, and beat into the eggs on low speed until no flour streaks remain. Beat in the chocolate mixture. Stir in the walnuts and the remaining 12 ounces chocolate chips. The dough will be very soft. Cover the bowl tightly and refrigerate for 2 hours.

3. When thoroughly chilled and solid, shape the dough into 2 logs, each 1½ inches in diameter. Wrap tightly in plastic wrap to hold the shape, and refrigerate for up to 3 days. Or, shape the dough into 48 walnut-size balls with your hands, place in a plastic freezer bag, seal tightly, and refrigerate for up to 3 days or freeze for up to 1 month.

CONTINUED ON PAGE 178

CONTINUED FROM PAGE 177

4. When ready to bake, place an oven rack in the middle position of the oven. Preheat the oven to 375°F. Line a 13×18-inch baking sheet (not nonstick) with parchment paper. Cut twelve ½-inch-thick slices from the log and place on the baking sheet; or place 12 walnut-size balls on the baking sheet.

5. Bake for 10 to 12 minutes or just until the cookies look shiny and the crust starts to crack. Cool the cookies for 2 minutes on the pan; then transfer to a wire rack to cool completely. Repeat with the remaining dough.

Storage: *Refrigerate leftovers, tightly covered, for up to 3 days or freeze for up to 1 month.*

PER COOKIE: 110 calories; 2g protein; 7g total fat; 1g fiber; 13g carbohydrates; 15mg cholesterol; 22mg sodium

No-Cook Chocolate Cheesecakes

MAKES: 6 SERVINGS   PREPARATION TIME: 5 MINUTES   CHILLING TIME: 1 HOUR

It is much easier to serve cheesecakes in little wineglasses than to cut slices from a large cake. This recipe requires no baking, so it is super-quick. (Although they need to chill for at least an hour before serving, you're free to do other things.) Vary the fruit preserves topping as you like.

- ¾ cup gluten-free chocolate syrup
- 2 tablespoons honey or agave nectar
- 1 teaspoon pure vanilla extract
- ⅛ teaspoon salt
- 2 cups light whipped cream or whipped topping
- 1 (3-ounce) package light cream cheese or cream cheese alternative, at room temperature and cut into 8 pieces
- 3 teaspoons apricot preserves or orange marmalade
- 4 mint sprigs, for garnish (optional)

1. Stir together ½ cup of the chocolate syrup, the honey, vanilla extract, and salt.

2. In a large bowl, place 1½ cups of the whipped cream. Add the cream cheese pieces and beat with an electric mixer on low speed until smooth. Gently fold the chocolate syrup mixture into the whipped cream mixture until there are no streaks. Divide it evenly among six wine glasses. Chill for at least 1 hour before serving, or make them the day before and refrigerate overnight.

3. To serve, top each cheesecake with 2 teaspoons of the remaining ¼ cup chocolate syrup, then a dollop of the remaining whipped cream. Garnish each with ½ teaspoon apricot preserves and a sprig of mint, if using.

Storage: *Refrigerate leftovers, tightly covered, for up to 2 days.*

PER SERVING: 382 calories; 4g protein; 27g total fat; 1g fiber; 34g carbohydrates; 96mg cholesterol; 173mg sodium

Vanilla Pudding

MAKES: 4 SERVINGS   **PREPARATION TIME:** 5 MINUTES   **CHILLING TIME:** 2 HOURS

Eat this pudding as is for a simple treat, or dress it up with fresh fruit toppings or use it in the Black Forest Trifle on page 184. It is so versatile that you will find many uses for it. To vary the flavor, replace the vanilla extract with 1 teaspoon pure almond extract or imitation rum or brandy extract.

- ½ cup sugar
- 3 tablespoons cornstarch*
- ¼ teaspoon salt
- 2 cups milk of choice
- 2 large egg yolks
- 1 tablespoon butter or buttery spread
- 1½ teaspoons pure vanilla extract (light-colored, if possible, for a lighter-colored pudding)

1. In a medium, heavy saucepan, whisk together the sugar, cornstarch, and salt until well blended. Before placing the pan on the heat, gradually whisk in the milk and egg yolks until very well blended. Cook over medium heat, whisking constantly, until the mixture starts to boil. Then cook for 30 seconds more, whisking constantly as it thickens.

2. Remove from the heat; stir in the butter and vanilla until thoroughly blended. Cool for 10 minutes in the pan, and then pour into a serving bowl or four individual dessert bowls. Press a sheet of plastic wrap directly on the top(s) to prevent a skin from forming. Chill until firm, about 2 hours, before serving.

Storage: Refrigerate leftovers, tightly covered, for up to 1 day.

PER SERVING: 230 calories; 5g protein; 7g total fat; 0g fiber; 37g carbohydrates; 119mg cholesterol; 200mg sodium

* Use 4 tablespoons cornstarch if using low-protein milk such as coconut, sunflower, or rice, or else the pudding won't thicken properly.

Chocolate Pudding

MAKES: 6 SERVINGS   PREPARATION TIME: 10 MINUTES   CHILLING TIME: 2 HOURS

Serve this elegant yet simple dessert in special glasses or espresso cups as the perfect ending to a dinner party. Top with a dollop of whipped topping, a dusting of cinnamon, fresh strawberries, chocolate-covered espresso beans—or whatever strikes your fancy. You can also vary the optional liqueur by using hazelnut or mint liqueur in the same amount.

    3 tablespoons unsweetened Dutch-processed cocoa powder
    ¾ cup packed brown sugar
    3 tablespoons cornstarch*
    1½ teaspoons instant espresso powder (optional)
    3 cups whole milk of choice
    2 ounces gluten-free chocolate chips
    ¼ teaspoon salt
    1½ teaspoons pure vanilla extract
    1 teaspoon orange or almond liqueur (optional)

1. In a medium saucepan, whisk together the cocoa, brown sugar, cornstarch, and instant espresso (if using) until well blended. Turn the heat to medium, whisk in the milk, chocolate chips, and salt, and cook, continuing to whisk until the chocolate melts and the mixture thickens, 5 to 8 minutes.

2. Remove from the heat and stir in the vanilla and liqueur, if using. Pour into a serving bowl or four individual dessert bowls and press a sheet of plastic wrap directly on the top(s) to prevent a skin from forming. Chill until firm, about 2 hours, before serving.

Storage: *Refrigerate leftovers, tightly covered, for up to 1 day.*

PER SERVING: 340 calories; 7g protein; 7g total fat; 2g fiber; 66g carbohydrates; 7mg cholesterol; 245mg sodium

* Use 4 tablespoons cornstarch if using low-protein milk such as coconut, sunflower, or rice, or else the pudding won't thicken properly.

Superfast Polenta Pudding

MAKES: 4 SERVINGS   PREPARATION TIME: 2 MINUTES   COOKING TIME: 20 MINUTES

Traditional polenta requires standing over a stovetop . . . and stirring, stirring, stirring. Instead, this quick microwave method frees you up to do other things. Deliciously flavorful apple butter replaces several ingredients to help speed up preparation. For breakfast the next morning, warm up any leftover pudding, and top with yogurt.

- 3 cups milk of choice
- 1 cup Bob's Red Mill gluten-free yellow polenta/corn grits
- ⅛ teaspoon salt
- ¾ cup apple butter
- ¼ cup dried cranberries
- 1 teaspoon pure vanilla extract
- 6 tablespoons whipped topping, whipped cream, or Greek-style plain yogurt
- 2 tablespoons sliced almonds

1. Whisk together the milk, polenta, and salt in a large microwave-safe bowl. (I use an 8-cup Pyrex measuring cup, which is large enough to avoid boil-overs.) Lay a sheet of waxed paper over the bowl and cook in the microwave on High power in 10-minute increments, whisking between each increment. Cooking times may vary depending on your microwave. Mine takes two 10-minute increments, for a total of 20 minutes, but yours may take more or less time.

2. Stir the apple butter, 3 tablespoons of the cranberries, and the vanilla into the hot polenta until smooth. Serve immediately in four small bowls or glasses, dolloped with whipped topping and sprinkled with the almonds and remaining 1 tablespoon cranberries.

Storage: *Refrigerate leftover pudding (without the whipped topping), tightly covered, for up to 1 day.*

PER SERVING: 385 calories; 11g protein; 7g total fat; 6g fiber; 71g carbohydrates; 1mg cholesterol; 162mg sodium

POLENTA OR CORN GRITS?

I prefer Bob's Red Mill gluten-free polenta/corn grits (the package is labeled with both names) for this recipe because of its gorgeous yellow color, stone-ground quality, and, of course, safety (their dedicated gluten-free facility). If you use other gluten-free brands, the degree of processing and coarseness may require you to adjust the cooking time accordingly.

Black Forest Trifle

MAKES: 12 SERVINGS   PREPARATION TIME: 15 TO 20 MINUTES

This elegant dessert may seem complicated, but it is quite simple to make. Yet, the presentation is impressive, so your family or guests will likely be asking for more! Obviously, it comes together quicker when the ingredients are ready-made or store-bought, rather than starting from scratch.

- 1 9-inch pan store-bought gluten-free chocolate brownies (or Chocolate Brownies, page 173)
- 1 tablespoon cherry brandy (optional)
- 1 (14.5-ounce) can cherry pie filling
- 4 cups whipped cream or whipped topping
- 2 cups store-bought gluten-free vanilla pudding (or Vanilla Pudding, page 180)
- 1 (11-ounce) can mandarin oranges, drained and patted dry
- 2 tablespoons unsweetened Dutch-processed cocoa powder
  Fresh mint leaves, for garnish (optional)

1. Cut the brownies into 1-inch pieces and place half in a layer on the bottom and along the sides of a straight-sided glass bowl or a 9-inch glass trifle bowl.

2. Stir the cherry brandy (if using) into the cherry pie filling and spoon all but 1 tablespoon over the brownies. Smooth the cherry filling with a spatula and press the filling firmly against the sides of bowl to create a visible layer.

3. In a large bowl, fold the whipped cream into the pudding, and then spread the mixture evenly over the cherries and firmly against the sides of bowl to create another visible layer.

4. Place the remaining brownies around the edge of the bowl, creating a ring of brownies around the top. Inside the ring of brownies, arrange a ring of mandarin oranges next to the brownies.

5. To serve, garnish the top with the remaining 1 tablespoon cherry pie filling. Dust with the cocoa and garnish with mint leaves, if using. Serve immediately.

Storage: *Refrigerate leftovers, tightly covered, for up to 1 day.*

PER SERVING: 455 calories; 6g protein; 27g total fat; 3g fiber; 53g carbohydrates; 89mg cholesterol; 279mg sodium

Chocolate Mousse

MAKES: 4 SERVINGS   **PREPARATION TIME:** 5 MINUTES   **CHILLING TIME:** 1 HOUR

This is probably the simplest mousse you will ever make. Serve it plain and let it speak for itself, or top it with some colorful fruit or raspberry or strawberry preserves. Whipped cream or whipped topping is a classic garnish, but you could use dollops of lightly sweetened yogurt instead.

   ¾ cup gluten-free chocolate syrup
    2 tablespoons honey or agave nectar
   ½ teaspoon pure vanilla extract
   ⅛ teaspoon salt
  2½ cups whipped cream or whipped topping
    4 teaspoons raspberry or strawberry preserves (optional)

1. In a small bowl, stir together ¼ cup of the chocolate syrup, the honey, vanilla, and salt.

2. In a large bowl, place 2 cups of the whipped cream and gently fold in the chocolate mixture until there are no streaks. Divide the mousse among four serving glasses or bowls. Chill for at least 1 hour.

3. To serve, top each serving with 2 tablespoons of the remaining chocolate syrup, then 2 tablespoons of the remaining whipped cream. Top each with 1 teaspoon fruit preserves, if using.

Storage: Refrigerate leftovers, tightly covered, for up to 2 days.

PER SERVING: 390 calories; 3g protein; 24g total fat; 1g fiber; 49g carbohydrates; 83mg cholesterol; 125mg sodium

Sources

National Associations

Several nonprofit associations provide a wealth of information on the gluten-free lifestyle, including newsletters, magazines, and Web sites. Many hold conferences and also sponsor support groups in many cities, so check to see if one is in your area.

American Celiac Disease Alliance
www.americanceliac.org

Celiac Disease Foundation
www.celiac.org

Celiac Support Association
www.csaceliacs.org

Gluten Intolerance Group
www.gluten.net

National Foundation for Celiac Awareness
www.celiacentral.org

Magazines

These lovely, color magazines are available by subscription. Some can be found on magazine stands.

Easy Eats
www.easyeats.com

Delight Gluten-Free
www.delightglutenfree.com

Gluten-Free Living
www.glutenfreeliving.com

Journal of Gluten Sensitivity
www.celiac.com

Living Without
www.livingwithout.com

Simply Gluten-Free
www.simplygluten-free.com

Universities and Medical Centers

Many universities and medical centers have established research centers that conduct research, diagnose patients, hold conferences, and offer a wealth of information on their Web sites.

Celiac Center at Beth Israel Deaconess Medical Center
www.bidmc.org

Celiac Center at Paoli Hospital
www.mainlinehealth.org/paoliceliac

Celiac Disease Center, Columbia University
www.celiacdiseasecenter.columbia.edu

Celiac Disease Clinic, Mayo Clinic
www.mayoclinic.org

Center for Celiac Research, Massachusetts General Hospital
(formerly at the University of Maryland)
www.celiaccenter.org

Jefferson Celiac Center
www.hospitals.jefferson.edu/departments-and-services/celiac-center

University of Chicago Celiac Disease Center
www.cureceliacdisease.org

William K. Warren Medical Research Center for Celiac Disease, University of California at San Diego
www.celiaccenter.ucsd.edu

An excellent book that will help you understand the nutritional aspects of the gluten-free diet is *Gluten-Free Diet: A Comprehensive Resource Guide*, **by Shelley Case, RD** Case Nutrition Consulting, 2013. Also visit www.glutenfreediet.ca.

Index